PATHWAY
TO A
POSITIVE
MENTAL
ATTITUDE

17 Steps to Success
Conversations with World-Class
Napoleon Hill Certified Leaders

Featuring
Lefford Fate

Special contributions by Don Green,
Executive Director of the Napoleon Hill Foundation

Table of Contents

Foreword

Lefford Fate, Napoleon Hill Certified Leader

Lefford, tell us a little bit about the Napoleon Hill Foundation.

Lefford Fate: Well the Napoleon Hill Foundation is there to help people. They're a non-profit organization to help grow and develop people; to help them to become more successful. They do that based on the Napoleon Hill Foundation mission of Making the World a Better Place in Which to Live.

One of the reasons I think Napoleon Hill's books were so great was because they were so foundational. Andrew Carnegie got with young Napoleon Hill and asked him to interview the top men in the country to find out what they knew to help people become successful. His thoughts were that it doesn't matter what social economic path you came from, where you came from, or what color you were. it is a way for any person who wants to be successful to follow these success principles and they can go from where they start to wherever they want to be. I think the reason it was so well received was because success leaves clues.

So, he went out there and interviewed 500 people that were the top of the top.

These are time-tested principles and the strategies were proven repeatedly and it became a rock-solid foundation. I think every motivational guru today, from Tony Robins to Brendon Burchard to John Maxwell to whoever you want to talk to, they started with Napoleon Hill's principles.

As a Napoleon Hill Certified Leader, what does that entail and what words of encouragement would you give to others considering becoming one as well?

Lefford Fate: Well, a Certified Leader, basically what you're doing is you're going to the roots. You're going to the roots to study where it came from and the principles behind those teachings. I wanted to get down to the bottom and understand the Principles behind the actually Principle, and that's one of the main benefits of being a Napoleon Hill Certified Leader, because you get to understand why they did it, where the research came from, how it's been effective, the tried-and-true practices and techniques to get to wherever you want to go.

Also, becoming a Certified Leader, I'm not doing it on my own. One of the main benefits is that I am surrounded and supported by world-class Leaders from the Napoleon Hill Foundation!

Let's talk about your project called, "The Pathway to a Positive Mental Attitude: 17 Steps to Success Conversations with World-Class Napoleon Hill Certified Leaders." Give us a little bit of background on your project and how you came to choose these world-class Certified Leaders.

Lefford Fate: Last year, I went to Wise, Virginia, to the University of Virginia at Wise, and went through the actual graduation process. I had been working with several of those leaders, and they went through classes with me, online. We'd been talking on the phone and we'd been basically masterminding on how we got through the process, telling our stories about how we became successful in life—because a lot of people talk about success, but they're not doing it.

I met those men and women from around the world, who became successful by walking certain paths. So, as I learned, and as they learned from each other, we just started developing relationships. Those relationships made me wonder if I could share these things with other people, with friends and family, especially. I'm a Military Veteran. I love airmen and their families, and I wanted to help them. So, I surrounded myself with that group of people and I asked them to join me in this project. We started talking about the pathways were and where the light is on our path to get to where we want to go.

I met people from Canada, from India, from Sweden, from America—from all over the world. We got together and said, "This is how we got here from there. We taught the Principles that Napoleon Hill followed. A Positive Mental Attitude is the key to get there, because if you don't think you can, you won't. If you don't use Applied Faith, if you don't put works into action you'll never get there."

We brought it together and we have this wonderful project called Pathway to Positive Mental Attitude and Success and I'm extremely excited about it.

If this were Lefford Fate talking about his personal perspective on each one of the 17 Principles, that would be wonderful, but you have stepped out of the spotlight and brought in these world-class leaders from literally around the world allowing them to bring in their life experience, business experience and experience with working with clients through these Principles. This brings deeper perspectives, not just yours!

Lefford Fate: I think that the Principles work for everybody, but there's a different perspective for everyone. Everybody's not an African American boy growing up in Georgia with a funny name that joined the Air Force and spent 31 years serving his country; that may not connect with some people. All of us need, in my opinion, somebody that looks like us, sounds like us, has those experiences to be able to relate to on one side. On the other side, we also need somebody that's a little bit different so we can see from a different perspective.

Bringing all these different people in, male, female, black, white, Asian, Latino, into this process, it gives everybody a little glimpse and understanding. To me, I think it was perfect and this won't be the last time we do this, because there are a lot of people all over the world that have a slightly different perspective and if we can understand others, we can understand ourselves better. That's what we need right now in our world - different perspectives on how to get to the right path.

I'm really excited about what we get to do in this project and that I've just been blessed to be a part of the process.

Learn more about the Napoleon Hill Foundation: https://www.naphill.org

Principle #1: Definiteness of Purpose – Interview with Grant Campbell

---

The development of definiteness of purpose is the starting point of all achievement.
~Napoleon Hill

Grant, why is the Principle of Definiteness of Purpose relevant for today?

Grant Campbell: Personally, I believe Definiteness of Purpose is as relevant today as it was when Napoleon Hill first penned that expression. Today, people are searching for meaning and wind up trying a variety of different things—a flavor of the month technique or solution—to find fulfillment, purpose, or even the why behind what they want (or why they want it), so this, being the first principle in the system is so very appropriate.

Napoleon Hill himself referred to this principle as the starting point of all achievement. That places a significant emphasis its importance as well as a concept that's referred to in some Eastern philosophies as the "beginning with the end in mind".

One of the things that comes through understanding and embracing this Principle is that specificity is required. When you talk about someone who specific about what they want and why in a particular thing or field, you're talking about someone who can develop a complete understanding and mastery of the most basic concepts—again, a point that both Dr. Hill and my personal teacher also emphasizes—repetition is the mother of skill. You can be a jack of all trades and a master of none. In this day and age, specificity is really one of the things that separates those that achieve outstanding results from those that just participate in doing whatever it is we're talking about.

Definiteness of Purpose in your mind helps avoids distraction and can help you focus your attention and efforts. It actually can make it so that you feel as if you're being pulled in the direction of what you really want as opposed to the feeling of having to exert all of this extra energy and trying to force things to happen. When you're clear about your beliefs as to why you're doing something or what you want, it facilitates the entire process and the entire system of doing things.

Sometimes there are opportunities all around us that we don't pick up on because we're just so all over the place and not focused, right?

Grant Campbell: Absolutely. A lot of experts will talk about going over your goals on a regular basis. Why would they say that? For exactly that reason.

The reticular activating system is a natural process in our brain that helps us to see things that are important to us and important to our survival. That's being utilized to draw us closer to our goals. We see opportunities that, if we were not focused or if we were not sure of our reason why (and had that passion), we wouldn't otherwise see. If we're not paying attention, we don't see those as opportunities when they appear. We might even see them as obstacles.

What misconceptions are out there, surrounding the Principle of Definiteness of Purpose?

Grant Campbell: One of the biggest mistakes that I see people make and why sometimes people become disillusioned is because they confuse the why of something with the purpose of it. They'll be confused about the difference between having a goal and having that Definite Purpose for their life. Having the purpose generally differs from goals, because goals are kind of like steps that are accomplished as you move toward what your purpose is. Purpose deals with your impact on others.

Purposes that are self-serving don't permit personal growth. They don't encourage fulfillment of the individual and they don't contribute to anyone else. So, a Definite Purpose should connect you to other people. Look at the answers to these questions: "What is the purpose of your life? What is your life's mission?" If your life mission is merely to make money, you're misunderstanding a goal for a purpose.

What positive changes did you experience in your life after applying this Principle to your personal and business life?

Grant Campbell: It's difficult to describe, because I feel almost as though I was exposed to these teachings so early on that fulfillment has never really been an issue for me.

Growing up, you're uncertain in many cases about which direction, what approach, and what system (if any) to take or use and how are you going to get "stuff" done. Once I understood how to apply my skills, how to apply and develop my passion, and to connect that to others, things just opened up. They just changed. I noticed that I didn't have the same questions that other people had. And that promoted an inner peace which for me lead to clarity and a sense of fulfillment.

I have friends and encountered people that have spent years doing everything they thought they were supposed to do, and then they got to a station in life where they wondered, "Is this all I get? Is this all it's about?" It's a confusing time. But I've been connected to other people my entire life and I knew exactly what I wanted to do, at the age of seven, so I did just that. I had a purpose in everything that I did. That doesn't mean things always worked out the way I wanted them to, but behind that was a sense of purpose and dedication to something that was much bigger than just me. It offered benefits to more than just myself. So, at times, when I felt down, it stood me up literally, and made me move forward.

That is something that I want to be able to encourage and help other people with, and explain more about that whole process, because I experienced that directly. The teachings of Napoleon Hill so eloquently put together the experience of developing your passion, commitment, and moving forward with your life—a life of purpose.

Can you share an example of how you have helped a client overcome these obstacles and succeed in using the Principle of Definiteness of Purpose in their personal or business life?

Grant Campbell: Absolutely. One reason I rarely even talk about my particular situation and my own sense of purpose is because a lot of people can't relate to that. A lot of people can't necessarily relate to someone that understood what's important in life early on, and I need to explain that a little bit. One of the things that I believe very strongly motivates all human behavior is pleasure or pain. Early on in my life, I had a lot of pain as a result of bullying and intense situations that happened as a result of my health when I was very, very young.

So, being in a situation where I couldn't do what other people could do, I was taken advantage of by others often. I knew that was wrong but was powerless to stop it. Once I discovered, at a young age, a system or the path by which to empower myself, it led me to a strong desire to empower other people. That's how that came about. I'm not like some prodigy that just had it all figured out at a young age. I was a kid that grew up in a very, very rough area of New York, and I was fortunate because I was able to take a negative situation and turn it into a positive.

Now, with regard to my helping other people, I've helped many people over the years. One example would be a kid who was on the wrong path back in the 90's. He had quit school, saw really no hope of doing anything other than living the street life, which includes drugs and thuggery and all kinds of things like that. This kid noticed that I was teaching other people and that I had a certain attitude whoever he saw me. He always saw how other people related to me, and he got involved in a conversation with me once simply because it was raining, we were both looking for cover from the rain in New York at that time. We were standing right next to each other.

What winds up happening is he gets into this conversation with me and I speak about what it is that I do. He asked me, "How'd you get into that?" I told him a little bit about it. Then I asked, "What do you do?" He says, "Oh, you know, I'm out here in the street, and I'm doing my thing." I said, real simple, "Why do you do that?" He gave me an answer, and I said, "Is that true? Is it true that you have to do that in order to make money and survive? Is that all you've got? Is that all you can be? You know the chances of you surviving to do something bigger and greater are really small. You know how that world works." I spoke to him from the heart. I just said, "You probably have more going for you than you're giving yourself credit for, and when you're really interested in being a little more than what you are right now, come and see me and I'll make time for you."

This kid wound up seeing me the next week, enrolling in one of my programs. Fast forward, years later, he's now a successful engineer.

I'm very proud of that. I still check in with his family, and they still get in touch with me from time to time. It's just been a whirlwind ride, being able to help people, and expose people to other options.

What specifically was it that inspired you to look at and become Napoleon Hill Certified Leader? And what words of encouragement would you give to others looking at potentially doing the same thing?

Grant Campbell: Well, that's simple. When it comes to the personal development field, there are a few giants and a few that have pioneered the field. Napoleon Hill is probably the most significant figure in the in the personal development field. From his teachings, many others arose. Many others have renamed it and they've put their own twist on it but it, essentially, is the grandfather of all the other systems of development that people have flocked to. I think there's no higher authority or a more proficient authority on the philosophy and teachings of Dr. Hill than the Napoleon Hill Foundation. When it comes to disseminating the knowledge and information of Dr. Napoleon Hill, I think it's a no-brainer.

If you're interested in applying the teachings and want to or think that you would want to share the benefits of it with others, I would encourage people to go to the foundation.

There's a big difference between knowing and doing, or just having a bunch of strategies and tactics. What do you think an implementation action plan is for this Principle?

Grant Campbell: Plans need to be kept simple. Something I teach to others is a Five-Step Action Plan for developing Definiteness of Purpose.

The first step is that your Definite Major Purpose must be important to you. It sounds pretty simplistic, but it has to really matter to you. It has to be something you believe in, something that you're committed to, something that drives you, something that must be. It's not something that should be, it's something that must be. And that helps you to develop the passion within you and also the strength within you that it's going to take to turn that into a reality. That's the first step.

Next, it should serve the people around you. You don't live in a vacuum. We already understand that we are designed to work together, as a species. We can get much further along in life working with others than we can by ourselves. So, your Purpose needs to connect with other people on some level.

Thirdly, your Definite Purpose should enhance your growth as a person, because that's one of the most basic needs that we all have, spiritually and otherwise—we need to grow as people.

Fourth, passion has to be an important ingredient in forming your Major Purpose. Passion creates the energy you need to get to that purpose.

The last step is simply to act on it. Do something about it. Don't just have goals, don't just have a purpose and not work toward it. It must be worked at diligently.

Those would be the keys to determining a Major Purpose, and having Definiteness of Purpose, as far as I'm concerned. You go through each step and if you don't know the answer, you don't leave it out. You can involve friends and you can involve other people that you trust. Those steps are key, and anyone that I've encountered over the years that has achieved outstanding results and lives a quality of life that they're proud of has done these five steps.

About Grant Campbell

Grant Campbell is an internationally renowned teacher, coach, a multiple business owner and author.

He's taught and coached thousands to achieve outstanding results in various areas of life. With a genuine interest in the growth and development of his clients that few in the industry possess, Grant truly lives and works with passion.

Learn more at www.grantcampbell.net

Principle #2 Mastermind Alliance – Interview with Napoleon Hill Executive Director, Don Green

---

No man can become a permanent success without
taking others along with him
~Napoleon Hill

Don, what would you say to someone that asks, "Why is the Mastermind Alliance a relevant Principle for today?"

Don Green: When, Napoleon Hill wrote the Laws of Success and published it in 1928, if you'll go look at it, it's over 100 pages, it's by far the longest Principle as for as the attention he paid to it, and I think it's because of the importance. We get asked that question a lot: Is his philosophy relevant today? I say the Principle of Success is compared to gravity. If you as a kid visit your grandfather, and you climbed up on his barn and you jumped off, you might've gotten hurt, you might've gotten killed. It doesn't matter when it happened. The law of gravity doesn't change. When you ask the question about is the Mastermind Alliance relevant today? Well, I read a lot of books. I read Steve Jobs' biography by the guy that wrote the book on the four geniuses. Walter Isaacson is his name. He wrote books on Leonardo Di Vinci, Ben Franklin, Einstein, and he finished it off with Steve Jobs.

Think about Steve Jobs and Steve Wozniak. They fit all the qualifications to be considered a Mastermind. They had one objective and of course we know what that was, the result is Apple, which is a trillion-dollar company today. If you study them, because I own their stock, they have about 250 billion in cash, their sales are close to 300 billion per year, and they employ many more than 100,000 people. That's as good as an example as you could imagine for the Mastermind Alliance.

If you want to think of another one, think of Microsoft: Bill Gates and Paul Allen. Another tremendous example of them meeting all the qualifications. Napoleon Hill defined it as "an alliance built with two or more people." He said, "Minds working in perfect harmony towards a common, definite objective." And, that's exactly what both of those people did.

Hill wrote in the Law of Success in 1928, "No one's ever attained outstanding success in anything without applying the mastermind principle," and I think that would be pretty hard to challenge today. I know that over 100 pages were written on the Mastermind Principle, the fact is, Napoleon Hill wrote more than twice what was written on most of the other Principles.

Do you feel like the Mastermind Alliance is like the concept of "Mentoring"?

Don Green: Yeah, there are some similarities, I mean getting along as far as teamwork or accomplishment and being in harmony. The difference is that in a Mastermind is everyone's mind should be attuned to the same objective. You can be mentor to someone, but they not have the same objective that you have. You can solve problems and so forth and work together, but I would not consider it a Mastermind because you could have five, six, ten, however many people working along together but they're not working for a common objective. They'd need advice, and maybe financial help. They have different requirements, but they also have different objectives. It would have parts of the Mastermind Alliance, but I wouldn't consider it a Mastermind because everybody involved must be like-minded and headed towards the same solution, the same ends.

Do you think some people would enter in and desire a Mastermind Alliance for their own personal gain? Should they focus on the reality that the Mastermind Alliance works only when everyone is out for the other members' success?

Don Green: Absolutely. But they also must be in harmonious cooperation, and getting along, and setting meeting dates, and learning from each other. That's cooperation or teamwork, but it doesn't fit the requirements of being called a Mastermind because of the simple fact that in a Mastermind, all minds are attuned. You could consider a medical group; their objective is to find a cure for cancer. Everyone is working toward the same end. They may have different contributions; somebody know biology, somebody know chemistry. But, still, they have an objective and that is to find a cure for cancer.

You know, I said it many, many times: people can learn from people. It's that simple. Again, a Mastermind is just one objective the group works on together towards a common objective.

What misconceptions are out there surrounding a Mastermind Alliance?

Don Green: Well, I think if you set out and you wake up one morning and you have an objective that you want to accomplish, I don't care what it is. You know, to start a Charter school or to start a cable TV company, you must select people that could contribute to it and their objective must be the same as yours; people that are sold on your objective.

You can imagine when Martin Cooper set out to develop a cell phone. He went to people for assistance and they said, "There's no use for a cell phone." And, that was IBM talking. Of course, then he went to Motorola and got assistance. It's finding something that you have a strong desire that you can accomplish and involve other people because one plus one doesn't equal two. One plus one can equal three, four, or a much higher number because of using different brains, different ideas, different talents of other people.

Don, what positive changes are experienced when people begin properly implementing the Mastermind Alliance?

Don Green: Well, you know, I've been in a banking business and I have plenty of examples. I have friends who started off with $25,000 with an objective that they would mine coal. They knew where coal was located, and they started taking steps, but their one objective was to mine coal at a profitable basis; that was it. None of them were coal miners but they selected people to work with them. These guys had one objective; to mine coal, and I know they sold out for just a little bit over a billion dollars, starting out with $25,000 in capital!

Having a strong objective, putting the parts together, it's a good feeling. I remember when we put the cable TV company together. I had the idea and I talked to an attorney of what the legal process was and the best way to set it up. We formed a group and the only objective was to offer cable TV at a reasonable price. How did we accomplish it? We put the money in, we didn't borrow any money. At the time, I looked at the financial statement of large cable companies and they were charging a ridiculous amount. We thought we could roll it out to a little town and pay for it. Basically, we charged exactly one half. We had no advertising whatsoever. We never took out one ad. We simply made it available.

If I hooked up Lefford, for example, and I said, "Now, Lefford, you've got this for $39. You've been paying $79," Do you think he's going to keep quiet? No! He's going to tell his relatives. He's going to tell a guy next door who's going to tell the other guy next door…and finally, you got everybody.

We went ahead and finished that one town. We did the second down. Then, we applied for a license for a third town and fourth town. Then, we were approached with an offer to buy us out, and the offer was so good that it was hard to pass up; so, we sold.

It was just an idea based on a common objective, which was affordable cable TV and that's it. Provide with these people, working class people, cable TV at affordable price. We were all working toward that same goal. It was just fun, really.

Don, what inspires you today about the future vision of the Napoleon Hill Foundation?

Don Green: Well, I've got probably one of the best jobs in the world! I'll be 79 on my birthday, and I absolutely love what I'm doing. If I'm not traveling, I come into the office and I will work, where I have ideas because work inspires me. This past year, we had 22 kids who had scholarships going to the University of Virginia, where we're located here on the campus and where I've served as a Board member for 19 years in a row. I'm a trustee and President of the University of Virginia Foundation Board, which is the fundraising part of the college.

Our students last year graduated with the second lowest debt load of any four-year college in the United States, so we raised a lot of money. I'm inspired by that.

And, we're doing business with approximately 500 publishers all over the world. Any given day, on an average day I will deal with probably a dozen publishers all over the world from big countries, with 20 + different publishers in Russia. 25+ in China. I counted them the other day. We had 31 in Spanish, but we also publish in Iran, Iraq, Afghanistan, you name it, Armenia, Belarus, Estonia, Slovenia, Slovakia, Cyprus, Greece. If a place exists, our books are there. That inspires me!

What are the starting points for someone to begin implementing the Mastermind Alliance?

Don Green: Well, Napoleon Hill tells us to have a Purpose. He said to set up a Mastermind. What for? I mean, you don't get together, drink beer and bet on ball games. You must start off with a Definite Major Purpose. Go back to *Think and Grow Rich* and look at the chapter on Desire, he gives you the six steps to riches. That's a very good start.

But, as far as the Mastermind Alliance, someone who wants to start must have a reason to do it. They've got to have a strong objective that it's worthwhile that they believe in. They can have tremendous results through a Mastermind Alliance, and that's the starting point.

Don, how would it benefit anyone to become a Napoleon Hill certified leader?

Don Green: To me, it gives you integrity. I hear so many people say *Think and Grow Rich* is not about money, but I'm sitting here looking at the first edition. On the cover, it has "for men and women who resent poverty." He said he wrote the book for the millions of men and women who were living in poverty and fear of poverty, so I think it's important.

I used to sit beside W. Clement Stone who was a billionaire. He used the word "action" at the time. In fact, I have a few of the little lapel buttons he printed that say, "Just do it." We swear that's where Nike got their logo from! But that's what he would say if he was discussing something or other. He'd say, "Well, let's do it." The word is "action"!

Hill tells us over and over, "When you have an idea, you make plans and you start." Plans may not be good, they may be weak or what have you, but you're never going to get anywhere unless you start.

What's lacking in most people's lives is that they attend these seminars, they go but never do anything they learn. They must pick out something that they get excited about, have a passion for, an objective, and then go do it. They need to select people and come together in a harmonious relationship with a common objective. It only makes sense that they'll accomplish a lot more with this Mastermind Alliance.

About Don Green

Don Green is the flagrant American business entrepreneur having built a successful savings bank, a real estate enterprise, and a host of other small and successful businesses in southwestern Virginia prior to his latest career with the Napoleon Hill Foundation.

As the Executive Director of the Napoleon Hill Foundation, Don Green has energized the works of the famed author with a host of new books by noted authors demonstrating how the principles of the late Mr. Hill work to advance the individual in network with others around the globe. He has demonstrated unique determination to expand knowledge of Mr. Hill's motivational work the world over.

But, moreover, Don is a new global social entrepreneur. He has become one of the leading evangelists of entrepreneurial self-help through the proper utilization of Mr. Hill's Keys to Success and Think and Grow Rich. He is accepting of nontraditional ideas, change, and foresight tempered and bounded only by positive action. He is a realist with visionary outlook.

Enduring values. A determined work ethic. A positive outlook. Creating opportunities where there were none before. These are the hallmarks of Don Green's leadership and legacy, and these are the characteristics that make him a worthy selection as the National Leader of the Month for March 2007.

Don is a goal-setter. He calibrates his goals and objectives carefully but routinely works with sound methodology with dedicated fever to achieve success. He appreciates those around him and their goals too. Don seeks to share in the vision of others and help them attain their aspirations in entrepreneurial endeavors if they have potential for positive impact.

Don takes great pride in working with younger adults seeking to better understand the principals of business entrepreneurialism and work ethic. Each year he spends an extended period of his time to assist Central Appalachian college students through scholarships.

Learn More: www.naphill.org

Principle #3: Applied Faith – Interview with Amanda Forslund

Close the door of fear behind you and see how quickly the door of faith will open in front of you.
~Napoleon Hill

Why is the Principle of Applied Faith relevant for today?

Amanda Forslund: Applied Faith is relevant for today because when you have a faith and apply it in your words and deeds, you can be, do, and achieve everything you want. It is one of the most important of the 17 Principles. If you have a faith in your ability and believe that everything is possible, then take action, you can achieve any goal you want.

Everything starts in your mind, in your own thoughts, and that is the way we all create our future. When you have faith, your confidence grows.

Visualize your goal as accomplished. See what you want to accomplish. Be specific, clearly see what you want to accomplish, and see it be accomplished. See how it feels. Enjoy it, the power of it. Feel it. See it clearly and hold this feeling in your mind. You communicate with your subconscious mind trough your feelings, and when your subconscious mind takes it as a truth, it will work twenty-four hours to make it true.

What misconceptions are out there surrounding this Principle?

Amanda Forslund: For many people, when they hear the word "faith," they relate it to religion. This principle has nothing to do with religion. This is a misconception because many people think that it is just enough to believe in God, Allah, Buddha, or something else and all problems are solved.

Just because you believe or say that you are believer doesn't make things happen. You need to believe, feel, and take action to get what you want. We communicate with our subconscious mind through our feelings. Through feelings or emotions, we are sending information to our subconscious mind about what we really want, what we are afraid of, or what we doubt. Our subconscious mind works for us and it works 24 hours a day to get us what we want. That's why it is important that you are clear about your thoughts and what you hold in your mind. The subconscious doesn't care if it is positive or negative - what you get it depends on which thoughts you choose to think.

The best thing is that you can CHOOSE your thoughts and what you are holding in your mind. You have completely control of it - it is the ONLY thing you have complete control over - and you cannot think two different thoughts at the same time.

Another misconception is that some people believe in destiny and they accept whatever life gives them, because they believe that it is God's will. Whatever they experience, they think God is testing them, to see if they are true believer. They think that they cannot do anything about it and that is the life God want them to have. Or they don't think that their lives are under their control, and simply say, "That's the way I am, and I cannot do anything about it." They strongly believe that and feel it like a truth, so the subconscious mind takes it like a truth as well and does everything it can to make it true. Then, when things go wrong, that person says, "I knew that," and so starts believing even more that it is his destiny.

What positive changes did you experience in your life after applying this Principle to your personal and business life?

Amanda Forslund: That everything is possible, that everything has a solution, and you can do and achieve everything you want, if you believe that you can. You need to be calm and believe that anything is possible. My faith attracts the right people and opportunities come my way.

My experience is that when I want something and believe in it, I don't need in that moment to know HOW I should get it - at the start, I just need to believe that it is possible, and then I will attract right kind of people and circumstances. I affect people to do things which benefit me, without violating their rights or manipulating them.

I have a very good example of that. I went to Cyprus in June 2018 for a property tour without the intention of buying something, because I didn't have much money. I wanted to do that trip because I was curious and needed a vacation. I had never been to North Cyprus before, but I canceled my skin therapist course and followed my intuition to fly to North Cyprus. On the first day of the property tour, I found my dream house. When I saw it, I just felt it was mine and I must have it. It was a 105 square-meter penthouse, 100 meters from the sea, and I saw myself looking at the sunset in the evening, sitting there with a man I love.

I was single when I went to Cyprus. I felt in my whole body that this dream will come true, and I decided to buy it, without knowing how I would get so much money. The same evening, our Stockholm group was at the Carrington restaurant for dinner. I went to the bar to buy a bottle of sparkling water and when I came back, a Swedish man was sitting in the chair next to mine. We start to talk and find out that we have so much in common. Personal development was the theme. We talked the whole evening and we wanted to see each other more. We had so much to talk about. The whole week, every day, Mikael and I took a morning walk at 6:15 AM, talked about personal development, and then swam in the sea. We liked each other a lot but, for a reason, we couldn't be together.

At home in Stockholm, I tried to fix the first payment of $105,000 USD. I could borrow $60,000 from the bank. I had $10,000 USD, my daughter had $15,000 USD, and the rest ($20,000 USD) was impossible to get. Suddenly, Mikael ask me if he could help me with that. I didn't want him to, because I knew him only two weeks. It was very unusual that he offered his help because Swedish people don't loan money easily. But after I tried everything and couldn't get the money, I asked him to lend it me. So, the first impossible task was solved. The next payment of $14,000 USD would be in three months and I had no idea how I should solve it, but I did it, and I did it for the next one, and the next. All that time, I never lose faith that I will solve the money problem somehow, despite that it was very dark sometimes, but my faith changed the circumstances and my brain got creative to give me a solution. I will tell more about that in my coming book, which I will finish in 2020.

Can you share an example of how you have helped a client overcome these obstacles and succeed in using this Principle in their personal or business life?

Amanda Forslund: A very good example is Ztina, a girl who was always struggling with money and to support her family. Whatever she wanted to do it was always a lack of money that was the issue. Then she starts to work with me, and I spoke about Applied Faith. I told her that if she wants something, she needs to throw away all doubt and fear and just believe that she will get it somehow.

"For now, it is not important to know how you will get it. It is important to want it strongly enough and believe that you will get it, and then start to think how you should get it," I said.

Ztina tried with small things and was very surprised how quickly she was proven that it works. And when it worked on several things, she started to strongly believe in everything I told her. So, she tried something bigger. She started to think that she so badly wanted a MacBook Pro. I didn't know about that, but I got an idea in my business that it should be very profitable to make an online course about nail extensions, and then I was thinking about Ztina, because she is very good at that and maybe she can video record this course and put it together in Final Cut Pro. I didn't tell her anything. I just bought a MacBook Pro and gave to her one evening when all the students went home. She started to cry. Through her tears, she explained to me that she so badly wanted to have a MacBook Pro. All her doubts were gone, and she realized what power there is lying in faith and how important this principle is. That's why I am often saying that you can "manipulate" people without violating their rights. She wanted it, I got an idea, and we both were happy about that.

What inspired you to become a Napoleon Hill Certified Leader?

Amanda Forslund: I found the book *PMA Science of Success* on the Internet, and when I started to read it, I felt like I found a gold venue and I wanted to dig deeper. I was obsessed with that book; I couldn't keep it for myself. I wanted to share it with everyone I knew. I must teach those principles. So, I started to Google it, to find the owner of this book and make a deal and could start educating others on using those principles in their lives. I found the Napoleon Hill Foundation and the three steps course to be certified teacher. I was ready to pay much more money for this course, but it was so cheap that I couldn't believe it.

I started with home study in March, and then was to start the online course in June, but Step 3 certification was in May, so I jumped to Step 3 first and then did the online course in June. It was lucky for me to get this opportunity, because in this group, in

May 2018, I made new friends who helped me a lot on my way, and I met Lefford Fate, who started this book project with our classmates.

This group of students, especially five of them, Enette, Lefford, Surrender, Sandra and Alejandro encouraged me, and lifted me up and made me to believe that my power is unlimited. My courage and my confidence grew, and at the end of course I was so happy because I found my mission. I wanted to teach those principles and continue Napoleon Hill's legacy, spreading it into Europe. So, instead, to be certified I even bought a license for both Sweden and Croatia to teach those success principles. I am so privileged to be the first and only who got certified in those both countries. It is huge!

What is the 5-step implementation action plan for the Principle of Applied Faith?

Amanda Forslund:

Step 1: Write down your goal and believe that you can and will get it.

Step 2: Express gratitude many times daily for having already received what you want.

Step 3: Keep your mind open for hunches, and when you get it, take action at once!

Step 4: When defeat comes, see it as challenge and opportunity to learn and grow.

Step 5: Start where you are, knowing that what you have is plenty enough.

About Amanda Forslund

Amanda Forslund is a proud certified instructor of Napoleon Hill's philosophy science of success, business coach, passionate writer and public speaker. Amanda is founder and CEO of Millionaire Mind University a company which works with reprograming the mind, and has developed a training program, *Life by Design* to empower women to find and follow their passion and to reach theirs higher potential.

Previously Amanda had created a 7-figure beauty business in Sweden. Her mission is to continue to promote Napoleon Hill's legacy and spread his proven system of success into Europe. Amanda Forslund is privileged to be the first and only Napoleon Hill's certified instructor in 2019 in both Sweden and Croatia with exclusive right to teach those success principles. She has studied at Brian Tracy's Leadership program, certified at Steven R. Covey's course, *The 7 Good Habits*, and just attend the World Class Speaker 2-years mentorships program with Kane & Alessia Minkus.

But life wasn't always like that. Amanda grew up in the little village of Otok, in Croatia, together with her parents and 12 siblings. She quit school at the age of 14, working at jobs, tired of poverty and with a burning desire to be rich. According the bank account, Amanda still not rich in money, but she is wealthy. She has found peace of mind and inner happiness which she teaches at Millionaire Mind University.

Amanda strongly believes in the potential of individuals, unlimited resources within, and her goal is to empower women to dare to believe in themselves, change their mindset and encourage them to create the life they deserve.

Apart from her professional work, Amanda is a mother, grandmother, has a loving relationship with an amazing gentleman, and lives in Stockholm, Sweden. Amanda loves morning walks in the wood, reading, writing, meditates daily, and travels several times a year to her paradise island of North Cyprus; there she has a beautiful penthouse by the sea.

At www.amandaforslund.com you can find Millionaire Mind University's training program *Life By Design* with the step-by-step guide to get you where you want to be. This program will completely change your mindset and build your courage to dare to believe in yourself, find your passion and live the life you deserve.

Principle #4: Going the Extra Mile – Interview with Happy Bains

Going the Extra Mile will bring you to the attention of those who can provide you with opportunities and it will inspire you to move on your own personal initiative.
~Napoleon Hill

Why is the Principle of Going the Extra Mile relevant for today?

Happy Bains: Thanks for asking this preeminent question. It's one of my favorite Principles. Actually, it relates to my personal own story and how I realized Going the Extra Mile is a principle and is the way of matter where we can reap the rewards for our good service and become proud of what we provide to the beautiful world.

It goes back to when I was eight years old, when I started earning my first, not a salary, but money. My uncle used to have a bicycle. One day, I washed his bicycle. In the evening, he gave me five cents and I said, "Why did you give me that?" And he said, "Oh, I noticed that you washed my bike."

The next day I did the same thing without him asking me to do it, and got five cents, like the first time. Then I did again on the third day, and I got another five cents. But on the fourth day, I got nothing. So, I said, "Uncle, why did not give me five cents today?" He said, "My dear son, you did not wash my bicycle." I said, "Oh, interesting."

On the fifth day, I shined his bike like it was brand new—spokes, frame and wings and everything. He gave me ten cents that day, so I asked my uncle, "Why did you give me ten cents today?" He said, "You went above beyond to shine and sparkle my bike, so you get five cents extra." Since then, I got that concept, the idea of Going the Extra Mile.

I said, "If you do your best—not the best, but the excellent— you get the excellent rewards." One of my favorite quotes is, "When we do excellent service, we reap excellent rewards. And we do poor service, we reap poor rewards." There is nothing cheated in that. Since then, I have been practicing the Going the Extra Mile principle. Then, without asking, if we do our best with courtesy to provide the best service, best love, best respect, and treat each person as a very important and unique person and a little extra, it comes back in an abundant way. Every person on planet earth liked to be respected and recognized if we give them both, ultimately, we will get the same in returns. Everybody feels happy.

Today, a lot of people have a lack of self-discipline in daily discipline, specifically lack of self-discipline in eating, sleeping, smoking, drinking and sex. They want the rewards right away, so they don't go the extra mile. The most common habit of today's young people and most of the people is lack of self-discipline, persistence and consistency. They don't want to go the extra mile; they want to reap the rewards right away. They want to sow now and start the harvesting in the morning. The joy of serving others with positive mental attitude is the key to success!

Do you feel that sometimes the younger generation today has that attitude and feel entitled that they deserve more than the work that they've put out?

Happy Bains: Definitely. We live in the era of a mind era. It has been said that, in the last 5,000 years of civilization, what we have achieved in the last 100 years is our creative, innovative brainwork, which is a remarkable thing. If you use your golden mind in smart way, you should get rewarded in an excellent way.

Younger generation must understand that having a definite major purpose in life is the starting point of all individual achievements, the purpose of education is the excellent life. The good education and specialize knowledge make us more valuable to human society and the world will pay us more for what we do because we have taken our time to own our skills.

By using that principle of receiving the reward faster, especially for young people, they need to understand what they are creating. Not competing. When you research, invent, create and perfect something uniquely, they deserve more and unique rewards in their life for that. Nothing comes easy. If they want a faster and faster reward, they need to understand the most important decision they will ever make, is their number one success factor is their choice of occupation their vocation the work they will propose to do for others so that those others will provide with excellent rewards they deserve and need to live the kind of life they want to live. They need to put more hard and smart work, lot of people skills, networking, invention, creativity, and consistency. And it won't come overnight, that's for sure.

What have you found are misconceptions surrounding this Principle of Going the Extra Mile?

Happy Bains: If I do more and give more of my time, why not give more? Give more respect, give more value, give more time to the people, and empower ourselves more. The misconception with surrounding this Principle, especially around young people who haven't made any decision in their life since childhood, is that they don't know what they want to do after their school. They don't know what to do after their college and university. And when they go to job, most of the time they don't know why they are hired. They've always been told, so they're not taking initiative. They fail to understand this principle of Going the Extra Mile.

They think this is very easy, and there are tidbits online, and word-of-mouth. People have been marketing the things they should be not doing. Young people are like a copycat—they want to copy the principle, which works. But it doesn't work overnight. They think since this is the fastest thing, they can get it. Most of the time, they end up getting frustration, boredom and failure in that.

The unfailing solution is we need to remove the facts from the fiction and opinion. We need to gather practical proven facts from the suggestion/advice of the successful people, if you want faster success. If they want faster success, they need to put their head and heart and mind in that, to find the facts. If they will search toward the facts, they will realize that most—95%—people have an opinion. And opinion is the cheapest commodity on planet Earth. We need to stay away from vague opinion in order to become successful people.

You mentioned the story about your uncle and the bike, which was from your childhood. Have you noticed any positive experiences in your professional, adult life where you've applied Going the Extra Mile?

Happy Bains: Yes. It's very powerful, very meaningful for me since childhood. It's still with me; I can see that I'm washing his bike. With each individual service or client, in a personal way or a clientele way, I apply this principle, not to just give what they'd ask—I always put my creative part in that—but to see what extra I can do each time.

Every morning, when I'm dealing with my client or any personal service, I always ask one of my favorite questions, "How can I improve and grow my service today?" Then I just jot down some idea. I can do better than excellent than what I did yesterday. I'm always in the chase of competing with myself to bring the best and excellent service towards in personal and professional area.

Each time, I bring creative ideas and creative ways, and always in a positive, friendly way. Everything I do for my clients or for my beloved people, I always do in a positive and a friendly way, with my best tone and the best use of my vocabulary. I use that in my service, and it comes by naturally, and people love it. When you're real, they will see that in you, in your heart's voice, in your faith, and in your words, too.

The most important thing I want to say is that being resourceful is so important. If I'm resourceful, it can bring the best ideas, best answers, best concepts, and best way of doing things to my client and for my beloved ones and making their life easy. And I can get whatever I need.

Since childhood, I've realized it's not about what I want from the world, so, instead of saying "I want this from the world," we should be asking, "What makes me so special that I will do it to the world and they will shower to me with whatever things I may desire?"

With continue action, consistency and with a Positive Mental Attitude, Going the Extra Mile would be improving the same thing over and over and becoming an expert, like a scientist and doctor in your field, so that people may address you as an expert.

That's why experts write their own tickets/paycheque. That's why we stand in a higher bracket of the Success Pyramid, where we stand out, especially known for our skills and talents.

People who've been experts in their fields have the most rewards in their lives. They've been doing constant improving and bringing an implementation of new ideas in their fields. They don't put their head in ten different professions. Until they reach that stage when they achieve success in one area, then they can multiply it in different things.

As an example, Mr. Warren Buffet or Bill Gates didn't start with 20 different profession ideas or 20 different business areas. They started in one line of field. When they reached that stage, once they made their first million, the next million they would have made probably in 90% less time of that way they originally made it. So, focusing on one thing and giving the best and repeating the same principles and same discipline for the next project can be possible.

Giving our best shot has really helped me. I've been doing it since childhood, and I love it each second and each day.

You mentioned your personal successes, can you think of an example with a client of yours that that you coached, where you've taught them how to use the Principle of Going the Extra Mile and then, as a result, they saw a transformation in their life?

Happy Bains: Yes. I have dozens of case studies and realities. People can go on my main website or LinkedIn page and see what global clients are talking about. Specifically, there was a small village student from a different country and she just got a scholarship in one of the Vancouver University in Canada.

The lesson I taught her was that you not only need to study but you need to plan ahead about your future work, you need to have a vision that works a few minutes a day, and you need to Go the Extra Mile each day—not only learning about school books but also thinking ahead of time about which occupation you're going to work at. I advised her to start reading books on her dream job/occupation and writing down ideas, 10 ideas a day about how she can bring positive revolution. I also taught her, "How to improve your people skills and provide excellent service in your field"

I told her that the day will come where you will have thousands of ideas, and one idea can change your life.

Today, she is award winning student in British Columbia, Canada and reaping the excellent rewards globally by simply using the principle of Going the Extra Mile each day and she is empowering her village children for better and healthy future!

Most of the time, when we get projects, we start thinking at that time, but we need to think a little ahead of time about our fields or the jobs we have, or our businesses, or our clients. Thinking about a client you're going to meet or work you're going to do, and start your preparation early, because preparation is the key to success. Nothing can take the place of preparation and consistency.

A lot of my clients reap the rewards because I give them step-by-step plans to create a road map a blueprint. When they follow the principles, their rewards are definite. Some people get rewards within a day and some people get rewards within the month. It just depends how they take action.

I strongly believe Personal Initiative is the most important thing in our lives. People who listen to recordings or read books have taken one step, but what they going to do after that recording or book is over? Are they going to take some initiative on that some points they really liked, that made sense to them? The most important thing is taking action, taking a Personal Initiative, especially when you go to seminars and workshops, listen to lectures, and read books.

We get ideas every day. I get them in the air. That's what Thomas Edison said. He said, "Ideas are in the air." You just take one and perfect it.

And don't just do it at the minimum; do that extra bit so that you stand out. Anyone can do a task, and if you don't Go that Extra Mile, you then look like anyone else out there, your peers or your co-workers. But if you want your boss to look at you a little differently when you come in earlier, stay a little later, or do your job a little bit better, do not gossip or complain, you then are Going that Extra Mile.

What inspired you to become a Napoleon Hill Certified Leader?

Happy Bains: I'm glad you asked me that. First, it's an honor and privilege to be a Napoleon Hill Certified Leader where these Principle is over a century old. Going in, not many people know what these Principles are all about or what this secret formula is all about—which is no secret. These are simple things that've been adopted from all different sorts of people around the world—from Carnegie, Thomas Edison, Tata, Ambani, Warren Buffet, Gandhi, Mother Teresa to other dignified successful people from around the world.

What inspired me was that I wanted to empower young people for success, for massive success. I would like to say that creating a Definite Major Purpose at the age of 10 will lead you to massive success, and allow you to retire at the age of 30, instead of at 60 or 65. I'm an expert in empowering young people in that area and because I think there's a lot of room here to improve the groups for the coming generations and generation.

So, I took this initiative, coming from nowhere, started since age of 8 working in garage from being homeless twice (but I was not hopeless) to sleeping on park benches and railway platform benches, sleeping in hotel lobbies, polishing shoes, working in factory, cleaning home & office, to modeling, acting, fashion and event director to being a founder of GURU! GLOBAL CONSULTING LTD and now a proud certified Instructor at the Napoleon Hill Foundation. I had the vision and dream to become a global Certified Leader and grasp all the profound ideas and concepts and share them to the world, to those who are deserving and who are ready to learn something new to change their lives and others lives to make a better world for everyone.

I'm just doing my part. The only thing I have learned is that I'm still a learner. I don't proclaim or proudly say "I know everything." I'm just a learner, I'm a proud student. But I've learned what practically works, and I've gotten massive results with these Principles and secrets.

I just want to quickly share to people and don't want to take the credit. It's just about sharing the information out there, because there are a lot of young people who are deserving. They don't know, they don't have the right tools, information and direction. So, my humble mission is to just empower them. Until my last breath of my life, this is what I wanted to do since childhood. I think this certification has given me a bigger and broader channel and support to spread the ideas and secrets. This is a remarkable thing and I want to keep educating myself to bring the best formulas and secrets to provide to the world. It's an honor and privilege to be a Certified leader. Specially to empower youth and woman and all other people who needs my coaching.

What do you think an implementation action plan is for Going the Extra Mile?

Happy Bains: It's simple, there is no rocket science about this. Provide excellent service. Provide the excellent service and they will reap the excellent rewards. Find the positive motive behind your Purpose and do more than you paid for. Respect more, give more, and love more, from Day One, in both your personal and professional areas and do not judge people. It will come up in your character and attitudes and it will become a habit of doing more. When you do more, doing more becomes a habit because repetition is mother of habits. Each day do more in a creative and loving way.

Also, challenge the golden mind between your ears to produce more and creative ways of providing friendly and professional services—each time as the first time.

In order to achieve this Principle, there are four simple steps. If anybody applies them, they will get a massive self-healthy image and financial freedom as well.

First, we need to forgive all others with no strings attached. If we cannot forgive others, we cannot move ahead in life, because there are a lot of grudges in our heart and mind we keep in our day-to-day lives. We don't like this, or we don't like that man or woman, or the person or the country. Once we forgive others, we are making a lot of room in our heart and minds so that we can empower and bring more ideas.

The second step is we need to look at ourselves as the best. It doesn't matter where we are coming from, the immigrant or whoever we are, or if we have a proper English diction or accent. It doesn't matter. Do your best. Look at yourself as your best with full confidence, and the whole world will look at you in a positive way, too.

The third is to forgive yourself with kind eyes. We become so hard on ourselves that we tend not to forgive ourselves. We are human. We make mistakes. So, forgive ourselves with kind eyes and move ahead with a Positive Mental Attitude to do our best.

The last is not to worry about others, what others have done, or what others are doing. Keep up with your pace and don't feel guilty. March to your own drums, rather than marching on somebody else's. Every morning we have two choices—either we wake up with confidence or frustration. The choice is ours. And the intelligent way to is to choose confidence!

You can do it!

About Happy Bains

GURU! Has matured and prospered under the leadership of Mr. Happy Bains. Surrender's global nickname is "Happy." The name Happy was given by his mother who committed suicide when he was just four years old and during his teens, although he was homeless twice, but he was not hopeless!

Since then Happy has leveraged his broad experience in Youth and Women Empowerment, Lifestyle & Business development over 28 Million Dollars for his 'Global Clients' by coaching/consulting into an extensive international business network.

GURU! Is a licensed Canadian private firm by Mr. Bains and he is a certified instructor of the Napoleon Hill Foundation, USA. Mr. Bains has a heartfelt passion and mission to the empowerment and success of today's young people!

Learn More: www.guruglobalconsulting.com

Principle #5: Pleasing Personality – Interview with Happy Bains

---

Your personality is your unique trademark. It determines your success or your failure in selling yourself.
~Napoleon Hill

Happy, why is the Principle of Pleasing Personality relevant for today?

Happy Bains: Before I jump into the answer, it's very important for me to come back with my childhood story—why it is important for me, and why I think it's important for everybody. When I was four years old, my mom committed suicide and that was the biggest loss in my life. I ended up with a stepmom and later stepmom passed away with heart attack and then my dad got heart attack twice and I was bullied in my school and in community friend circle, then had hardships life.

But even when I was homeless twice, I was always dressed up. I looked sharp with a pleasing smile on my face. I was not acting like a victim and I was not blaming to the world or God, I maintained myself-discipline and did NOT indulged into drugs, alcohol, stealing, smoking or gang lifestyle. We always have the choice to maintain ourselves and present ourselves in a pleasing way—it's simple and the most important thing in order to become successful person. Even when a beggar is begging for money, why doesn't he beg for a decent shirt, pants or clothes so he can stay presentable? I mean, it's common sense. Beggar uses so much of skills and knowledge to write a sob story on the cardboard instead of writing a letter/resume and ask for a job or find a pleasing way to help others?

We are where we are because of our choices we had made till today. And we will become exactly what will think about most of the time!

The Principle of Pleasing Personality is very important for each individual to become likeable and a proud human being. Since childhood, it is very important for me. My global clients know me about my Pleasing Personality and many people admire it. This Principle means that you are always focused, ambitious, dressed sharp, you're smiling and friendly person, and have specialize knowledge in the line of your field and serving and respecting others with courtesy. And if someone want to improve Pleasing Personality, then take a 15 days' challenge to treat and respect every person as a most important person on planet earth.

Deep down inside our heart, we know that we can do that.

Now, coming back to the question, most of the people who are not highly educated or are poor have a lack of self-confidence. They do not believe in themselves, or in their self-image—their shape and size and color and country background. They try to fake it and wear a fake mask instead of using an inner Pleasing Personality trait.

So, we live in the age of time where you are constantly trying to do a lot of makeovers and stuff and we are trying to hide our inner qualities and "the real me" side. We need to understand the basic concept of Pleasing Personality doesn't come with a lot of money and or a lot of education or born in a rich country. It's right within us. We need to be real people. Most of us we are, but sometimes we fail to understand our inner qualities and inner strengths and fail to believe in ourselves.

So, having Definite Major Purpose in life, Positive Mental Attitude, Self-Discipline, Accurate Thinking, Teamwork, Going the Extra Mile, Personal Initiative, confidence and believing in one's self is the most relevant thing for today. We need to believe in ourselves—It's very important and simple to obtain the Principle of Pleasing Personality.

Do you feel that sometimes people allow the busyness of the day and the stress of the day to weigh them down, and that keeps their Pleasing Personality from coming forth?

Happy Bains: Yes, absolutely. Most people are living in a way of a copy-paste lifestyle, so, instead of creating or living the legacy lifestyle, they are just copying others and not living out their true selves or their dreams. For example, they think if I dress like this, or if I buy that car, then I'll have a Pleasing Personality. It is good to have a dream and material things, but stress should not carry the weight in a day-to-day lifestyle, in a rush of the time. Because we've been bombarded with so many opportunities and job tasks, we tend to forget that a time will come where we need to just give ourselves a mental and physical break. If we put one brick a time in each day toward our dream, there will be monumental results.

So, I believe we should not get into the rush of the "Go, go, go" thing. We should take time to reflect and do self-inventory each day about "What makes me special that I can do for the world? How can I improve each day? How can I be the best to my family, to my friends, and to my clients?" There are always challenges. All days are divided into three parts—eight hours of sleep, eight hours of work, and eight hours for ourselves. So, when we get our eight hours of work, we should put our heads and hearts inside our work to do the excellent work we can do. In the beginning of the career stage, if you're working twelve, fifteen, sixteen, or eighteen hours, it is good, but let's not get carried away— you have your own life and you can always have a Pleasing Personality rather than a fake mask you show to the world.

We are different people in media, and we tend to show things what we are doing which we are not doing. We're pretending. We have a different mask and personality in public. We have a different personality when are with friends and colleagues at workplace. We have a different personality when we come back home. We need to understand what exact role we're playing— what makes me special that I should be "the real me" so that my quality, my skills, and talent will be more appreciated than my physical appearance? If you go back in time and history, most successful people are not like superheroes, with six-packs and beauty and gorgeousness, they are simple people back there.

Mother Theresa had a Pleasing Personality. She was not a supermodel; what was a supermodel was her real self. It's a profound thing. And these kinds of things made me understand we all have the ability to appear, in any given time, with a Pleasing Personality. Our pleasing vocabularies and the smiles on our face are the biggest assets that we have.

Do you find that people that are not as confident need to take small, baby steps toward their confidence and maybe even act like they're confident, even if they don't feel like they're confident?

Happy Bains: In recent a recent media interview, I was asked, "Mr. Bains when did you become successful?" I told him I was successful and confident when I was homeless and sleeping on park benches because I knew what my burning desire is and I will get it anyhow, it's matter of time. Confidence plays a big role. I was so confident I could see where exactly I was heading in the world and what I'm doing, globally. So, I was confident enough to envision it, to visualize it. Goals are important but the most important thing is to have a vision it that keeps us going. Some people think we can borrow or buy confidence from others, but confidence is already inside us. Act enthusiastic and you will be enthusiastic.

Confidence is something that we need to develop each day. It's already inside us. We just need a little boost or push in being confident for what you are, what you know, what your language is, and what your country or culture is. Be confident about yourself. Don't try to pretend, change, or bring some additional mask on yourself. Be confident in the way you are with your family and friends. Be confident in the way in which you deal with your clients. The beginning stages will come with challenges that we will not have the answers for, but we need to stay confident anyway. Say, "You know what? I don't know the answer, but I know several other ways to find the answer."

Demotivating ourselves and lowering our self-esteem will cause our confidence to lower, too. Confidence is something that we need to practice. I think you should adopt role models in your life so that you can learn good things from those successful people.

So, we need to adopt some role models who are confident. But what makes them confident? The most important thing is we need to act, walk, talk, and behave like we are already confident. We don't have to wait to become successful, or say, "When I become a millionaire, then I'll be confident," "When I become a mom, then I'll become confident," "When I am a good student, then I'll become confident," or "When I have a good job, then I will perform well and be confident."

Let's not wait for the time in the future to create the image that you'll be confident once you obtain and achieve this. Confidence is right here— each minute, each second where you are—and it will come in your Pleasing Personality. It will show itself to the person who you're dealing with and they will follow and admire you. Most confident people are leaders, that's why the world follows the leaders—because they're confident. Imagine any positive leader in the world having no confidence. Would you follow them?

Every individual is a leader and they need to understand that the confidence is right inside, within them. They just need to bring it out. So, the idea is to act, walk, talk, and behave like you're already a confident person and you already have achieved your goals and vision—that you've already have what you want. So, visualize your future, then come in the present and act the part—that you are a confident person.

What misconceptions are out there surrounding the Principle of Pleasing Personality?

Happy Bains: Most of the people think that Pleasing Personality is the result of being rich or born rich, in a rich family, or being very highly educated, or born into an educated family or born in rich country. This is a myth. Pleasing Personality doesn't only fall in that category or areas. The misconception is that a Pleasing Personality can be in any area, shape, and form. Let's not get carried away and think that only successful people or educated people have the only rights to have a Pleasing Personality.

We are the molder and shaper of our own lives. We need to understand and create our own philosophy for the Principle of Pleasing Personality, but not create misconceptions that the Pleasing Personality is only for successful people or highly educated people. That image will destroy our confident self-image and we will never be put in a higher bracket of our life in a successful way.

When I was very young, in the olden days, my aunt used to have to cook food outside, using a fire she made herself. There were no gas stoves back then. I wanted to help but my aunt would not let me.

My aunt used to always tell me, "Good little boys don't do his elder adult's job. It's an adult's job."

Once I saw how she made the fire, I said, "When you start the fire to cook the food, you always usually put the small wood on first, not the big log."

She said, "Yes."

I said, "A small piece of wood can bring up a light to bring the fire to the big piece of wood, just like a small person or a small group of people can bring a new light to the world too."

It's important that not only bigger people can bring a successful light; young and poor people can also bring a new light to the world. This is a good lesson for everyone.

What positive changes did you experience in your life after applying the Principle of Pleasing Personality to your personal and business life?

Happy Bains: Always staying sharp is the most important thing at any given time. By staying sharp, friendly, helpful, and focused towards the Major Purpose of life, this Principle has enhanced my self-worth in the marketplace. It especially has had positive changes in my beloved one's hearts and minds because they see the effects and changes in that. Pleasing Personality is being friendly and being a good sportsmanship. Courtesy plays a big role, as does smiling, being tactful, being patient, proper dress, meditating, exercising daily and treating others as a most important person on earth.

We live in a world where what we wear is judged by others. People usually underestimate and they have a judgmental personality. I'm not saying all people are judgmental and they assume things but, for most of us, the minute you walk in any room, people judge us from our dresses, before we even open our mouths. So, it's very important that we need to understand where you are going, for which occasion, and to dress the part. Even if you cannot buy an expensive suit, you can still wear a good shirt and a pants—or a dress—that can be ironed in a sharp way.

Staying sharp was the most important thing when I was homeless, and that got me in a higher position, too. So, did staying focused and alert, and being helpful and serving others in a positive way. This is inner Pleasing Personality; we cannot buy all these things from outside, it's all within us. We just need to portray it and keep our talents on the table, and let the world choose and pick, and they will reward us what for what we want.

In my personal and business life, I've been doing my best in all these qualities—the inner quality combined with my specialized knowledge as a success coach. The world has rewarded me so much and I'm very thankful. I would be nothing without what world has given me—the credit goes to the whole world and the Universe. I have done my best and I have been rewarded because of my Pleasing Personality, which I maintain each second of each day.

Can you share an example of how you have helped a client overcome these obstacles and succeed in using the Principle of Pleasing Personality in their personal or business life?

Happy Bains: Yes. I have may young people —young students, especially. I coach and I do workshops and seminars for young people, especially. One of my students was very depressed and stressed and had a lot of anxiety and low self-esteem. I coached him and I told him that there are three most important things to do to get a massive result in your life. I told him to always get a good grade in school. The second most important thing is—and this message is for all young people—get a good job and stay in a vocation.

Now, a lot of times, what happens is that we drop out from school and get any job, in construction or a food court—which is okay at the ages of 15-18, but not when you are in your mid-20s and 30s. So, getting good grades and a good education is the most important thing, then you can find out which job you love, and then stay in the vocation that you want to do.

The third is not to hurry into marriage. When you have sizeable paycheck, you can get into that system. It takes only two minutes to get a marriage on paper, but to deal with that and to take the responsibility of parenthood and marriage is the very hardest thing—that's why most of the divorces happen—so, don't hurry into a marriage.

If we monitor successful people, we see these are the three best habits they have been doing since childhood.

My client listened to me and has received massive results— and he is not even twenty-five years old! He's very successful at his age and he has reaped the reward of his initiative and actions he took on this Principle and the suggestions I gave.

This suggestion can be taken by anyone. You just need to put it in order and follow the habits there. The ideas are all in the air. We need to pick and choose which one serves our purpose, and the world will reward us in a personal way and in a business way.

I have helped a lot of other people and told them, at any given chance, to do your best and stay out of drugs and the gang lifestyle. When we don't have anything, the fastest thing we can get into is the bad habits of drinking alcohol, smoking, doing drugs, and getting into prostitution and the gang lifestyle. It is very hard to stay persistent and obtain results in those hard way.

Since childhood, I had many choices to go into the gangster lifestyle, alcohol and to drugs, but I chose not to. I chose to stick to my Principles and discipline, to get educated first, to get the best job, and to do the business which I love to do.

So, a lot of clients—young students and immigrants—got the best results from my coaching, because I gave them a step-by-step plan. This blueprint to follow gives massive results within the first year.

What do you think an implementation action plan is for the Principle of Pleasing Personality?

Happy Bains: First, remove the facts from the fiction and remove the facts from the opinion. Everybody has opinions and we need to take a little time to listen to them, but then they need to remove the facts, and determine what exactly they said and if it makes sense or not. Gather the facts. And separate the facts into two parts, important facts and unimportant facts and use only important facts which takes you closer to your dreams and goals.

Having a Definite Major Purpose is the starting point of all individual achievements. Young people often don't have a Major Purpose in life and that's why they drift, and most of them will end up drifting in their old age, too. So, if you don't have a Major Purpose, the next step is to identify your Major Purpose of life. Even if you don't know what exactly you want to become in your life, that's okay. You can identify what you want to do this year or in the next six months or this month and take baby steps from there.

Seeking to your Major Purpose and burning desire towards your job or your business or your career will create a burning desire for other habits too as well. So, having a Major Purpose is very important and is part of the Principle of Pleasing Personality. And the persons who have a Pleasing Personality know within a minute what they want to do and become.

People should also understand that it's not important what are you getting at your job. It's very important what are you becoming at your job. It is also important in a relationship not to ask what you're getting from your relationship; it is very important to understand what you're becoming in your relationship. These Pleasing Personality traits should be applied in personal and professional ways, always to offer our best to our beloved ones and clients.

Next, write down ideas, your ten best ideas each day, about how you can improve your service or work toward your goal or vision. One best idea can change your life.

Whenever you have difficulties or problems, sit down, do not panic, and on a clean sheet of paper. On the left-hand side, describe the problem in detail. Define your problem using IF-THEN statements. For example, IF this will happen, THEN this will happen. Go to the depth of the problem, where the root of the fear is gone. On the right-hand side, write what you can do best about it.

Solving problems and challenges in this way will lead you to a higher level of thinking, and a higher bracket of success. Successful people are successful because they are doing the things that other people didn't do. It's very simple.

We all have greatness in us, we all have a Pleasing Personality, and we all have talents. We just need to bring them all outside. Being confident, being ourselves, staying sharp, staying focused, staying neat, meditate and exercise often, and staying clean are signs of prosperity. Cleanliness, in particular, is important. The cleanest people are the best people in the world. We can be the poorer people, but also, we can be the cleanest people. It's our choice.

**Always treat each person as the most
important person on planet earth!**

About Happy Bains

GURU! Has matured and prospered under the leadership of Mr. Happy Bains. Surrender's global nickname is "Happy." The name Happy was given by his mother who committed suicide when he was just four years old and during his teens, although he was homeless twice, but he was not hopeless!

Since then Happy has leveraged his broad experience in Youth and Women Empowerment, Lifestyle & Business development over 28 Million Dollars for his 'Global Clients' by coaching/ consulting into an extensive international business network.

GURU! Is a licensed Canadian private firm by Mr. Bains and he is a certified instructor of the Napoleon Hill Foundation, USA. Mr. Bains has a heartfelt passion and mission to the empowerment and success of today's young people!

Learn More: www.guruglobalconsulting.com

Principle #6 Personal Initiative – Interview with Napoleon Hill Executive Director, Don Green

---

Today's employer usually is yesterday's employee who found opportunities waiting for him at the end of the second mile.
~ Napoleon Hill

Why is the Principle of Personal Initiative relevant for today?

Don Green: You know, it's been said that "Sometimes our ship doesn't come in. You might need to swim out to where it is." In other words, you can create your own opportunities. I can quote word for word what Napoleon Hill quoted Carnegie about. He said, "Two types of people who never amount to anything." He said, "There are those who never do anything except what they're told to do, and then there are those who cannot even do what they're told."

I would relate a little story to you. I love stories. I got the Sam Walton Award one year for community work back when I was in banking. You got a cap with Walmart on it. Of course, I own Walmart stock, that makes me happy. I got his biography and there's a story in his book about Sam, he had a habit of paying visits to all his stores once a year, even when he got up to close to 1,000, he would visit them.

He went in one of his stores and he noticed there was a bunch of trash around the checkout. He told the manager, "This needs to get cleaned up." But the manager said, "We have a guy who comes by several times a day. He'll clean that up."

Sam goes to the back, he finds an employee, he says, "Where do you keep the brooms?" They told him. He gets the broom, comes out to the cash register, and sweeping and he cleaned it up himself. Do you think that guy might've gotten a lesson in personal initiative from Sam Walden himself?

In other words, if something needs to be done, you go ahead and do it without having to be told. It should've been a tremendous lesson for the guy. You'd hope that he learned something. And, I'm sure Sam meant to teach him that if you see something that needs to be done, you go ahead and do it.

In my lifetime, I've probably missed all kinds of things but I used Personal Initiative on so many accomplishments where nobody told me to do it, here's an example: I read Hills' material as a youngster and not only did I read his stuff, but I read what he read. I wanted to know where he got his knowledge from.

I thought, "We should recognize him." He's born right here, and if you travel to Virginia, you will see these historical markers everywhere, you know, "George Washington slept here" and so forth and so on.

I wrote a letter to a politician and told him I wanted to erect a historical marker to Napoleon Hill. I got a cute little letter back that said, "We don't recognize individuals." He said, "It has to be of historical significance, and they have to be dead 50 years," But, I didn't stop.

I got a friend to get me the list of about a dozen contacts and I started calling them. I basically got the cold shoulder. Then, one guy in Culpeper, Virginia, he was a clerk of the court and on the Board. I told him what I was doing. He saw me and he said, "I think that's wonderful." He said, "I read *Think and Grow Rich*, it's changed my life." He said, "I'll take this to the Board," and said, "You can consider it done." I didn't get it done as quick as I wanted to. It took me over a year, but when I did, it he became the only author in the State of Virginia recognized with a historical marker. And, it hadn't been 50 years.

I did some publicity on it and we had TV cameras, we had people from newspaper. They said it was the biggest unveiling of a historical marker since they've been involved. Today, I've had people come here from China, India, Korea, what have you. They want to make sure they have their picture taken at the historical marker, which is probably one mile from my office on a major four-lane highway.

Then, I told the state I wanted to put a stone wall around it just protect somebody running over it. They told me that I couldn't do that. Of course, I had to make some phone calls. Then, I was to ask them if they would plant grass and maintain it. They called me back and said it was stripped. That means they took the good soil out hunting for coal and grass wouldn't grow there. I got my brother-in-law who had a landscaping business. I said, "Glen haul me a few loads of top-soil down around that marker," so he did. So, I called the highway department back, told them I put down topsoil, I would appreciate it if they sowed grass on it.

Then, this guy, his name was Turner, he was Head of the Highway Department. He called me one day when I was in banking. He said, "Don, said they're giving me a dinner in two or three weeks," and he said, "They're going to honor me for my retirement, and I'd love for you to be there." I'm thinking, "I ain't got nothing to do with the Highway Department, why in the world?" But I told him I'd be there. At the dinner, they presented me a plaque. He introduced me, he said, "I want you to meet a guy, Don Green. He's the only guy that I know that doesn't know the meaning of the word no," and got a big laugh about it. I think that's a good example of Personal Initiative because nobody requested it, nobody told me to. I had the idea on myself and I did what it took to get it done.

Don, what misconceptions are out there surrounding the Principle of Personal Initiative?

One thing it cause you to do, if you've got initiative, you'll adopt a Definite Major Purpose. I mean, you're not going to sit there on the sofa and wait 'til somebody comes along and says, "Boy, have I got a good deal for you." It's probably not going to happen, but also, I think gives you a motivation.

You can be a success really easy if you really want it. Because, you might lack money, you may lack skills in certain areas, but if you have passion, you're really enthused about what you're doing, you have discipline, you will succeed.

I say that prisons are full of one type of people, and they're people that lack the idea of self-discipline. They can't discipline themselves, and they end up in a place where they're told what time they're going to go to bed, what time they're going to get up, when they're allowed to out, when they can take a shower, and what they are going to eat. All for the simple reason they could not discipline themselves, and they end up in a place that does the discipline for them.

If you really have initiative, I think you'll make prompt decisions because you can't just waiver back and forth like a tumbleweed and never make a decision. I know it in my own life it creates enthusiasm. It's been said a million times, if you love what you're doing, you'll never work a day in your life. It's unbelievable talking it to people that dread Monday morning. I mean, you know, I'm sitting here writing in my little pad listing a few things I want to attack the first thing in the morning, and I can't wait to get started. I love coming in Monday morning to see how many foreign countries tried to contact me over weekend. If you've got Personal Initiative, my God, it's contagious as all get-out!

I've employed lots of people when I was a bank president, and the one thing I would not put up with... I would put up with anything before I would put up with this, the one thing, which is a bad attitude. I don't want to be around those people because it affects other people. I guess, Mark Twain said, "Don't walk away from them people, run from them," because it affects you. And Personal Initiative does so much because you'll find yourself succeeding where other people went about something half-heartedly and will fail. It creates opportunities, it creates a future for you, and it also creates advancement if you're working for someone else. It's just an amazing quality to have to simply love what you're doing.

Napoleon Hill gave us examples, like the boy that went to work for Mr. Durant. He simply showed up to the first day of work, but when everyone else was leaving at five when the gong went off, as they called it, he went by Mr. Durant's office and said, "Mr. Durant, can I do anything for you?" He said, "Son, this your first day. Do you hear that gong? That means everybody leaves." He said, "Yeah, but everybody was in a hurry. I thought you could use something before I left. I'm not in no hurry." He said, "Well, I'm drawing some plans for a building. There's an office down at the end of the hall. Would you go down there and sharpen me a pencil?" He sharpened two, took them back. He made that a habit to go by Mr. Durant's office, said, "Can I do anything for you?" He was promoted within about six months, his name was Carol Downes, and he went around making speeches later on. He said sharpening those two pencils paid him somewhere between $10 and $12 million because Durant was the founder of General Motors and he gave, him stock because the company was just starting out.

Hill talked about the theory of compensation that Ralph Waldo Emerson wrote about, which simply was if you do more than you're being paid for, someday you'll be paid more than for what you're doing, and if you're not recognized by your employer, some other employer will steal you away. So many are people saying, "I'll start doing more when they pay me more," but they have it backwards. There's no reason for a raise if they're not producing. Just because someone has been on a job for a certain time, that doesn't mean they're entitled to a raise. If you're not getting promoted, there's no point placing blame on someone else.

Early in my career I learned that people can develop a thing called "blame", they will never succeed because there will always be someone to blame. "I don't have no money because my wife spends it. The kids don't help. They don't give me a raise. I'm underpaid." Go on, and on, and on.

That's the one thing I can enjoy about being successful. It speaks for itself. You don't have to go around telling people, "I got this, I got this, I got this, this, this." It just shows, it shows on your face and it shows the results of what out in connected to what you've done. You don't have to go around telling nobody that. They'll do it for you.

Don, how would you encourage someone to start applying Personal Initiative in their own life, so that they can realize these outcomes that you've been talking about?

Don Green: I think they will be surprised. I was 20 years old making $1.10 an hour and they called me "Hot-Shot" because of my enthusiasm and the way I worked. I didn't think of making $1.10 an hour, I just had read the books and I know that was just a starting point. They were giving me lessons I could study. I was reading the books. I was the youngest office manager in their history. I was 22 years old and I had guys working for me in their 40s and 50s because I had the enthusiasm, I was the first one to work and last one to leave, and I had it on my mind. I knew I was going to succeed!

Don, if you wanted to give someone two or three things that they can go out and do today to exercise Personal Initiative, what would you say that person should do?

Don Green: I've got a little sign on my table I sit at every morning and it simply says, "God, show me somebody that I can help today, in Jesus' name." And, I know that there will be, before the day is out, someone that I can help. It never fails, whether it's mentoring one of the young students, or recommending one of them for a scholarship, or writing a letter of recommendation for them, or whatever. I know there's someone that will come in my path that I can help before the day is out.

About Don Green

Don Green is the flagrant American business entrepreneur having built a successful savings bank, a real estate enterprise, and a host of other small and successful businesses in southwestern Virginia prior to his latest career with the Napoleon Hill Foundation.

As the Executive Director of the Napoleon Hill Foundation, Don Green has energized the works of the famed author with a host of new books by noted authors demonstrating how the principles of the late Mr. Hill work to advance the individual in network with others around the globe. He has demonstrated unique determination to expand knowledge of Mr. Hill's motivational work the world over.

But, moreover, Don is a new global social entrepreneur. He has become one of the leading evangelists of entrepreneurial self-help through the proper utilization of Mr. Hill's Keys to Success and Think and Grow Rich. He is accepting of nontraditional ideas, change, and foresight tempered and bounded only by positive action. He is a realist with visionary outlook.

Enduring values. A determined work ethic. A positive outlook. Creating opportunities where there were none before. These are the hallmarks of Don Green's leadership and legacy, and these are the characteristics that make him a worthy selection as the National Leader of the Month for March 2007.

Don is a goal-setter. He calibrates his goals and objectives carefully but routinely works with sound methodology with dedicated fever to achieve success. He appreciates those around him and their goals too. Don seeks to share in the vision of others and help them attain their aspirations in entrepreneurial endeavors if they have potential for positive impact.

Don takes great pride in working with younger adults seeking to better understand the principals of business entrepreneurialism and work ethic. Each year he spends an extended period of his time to assist Central Appalachian college students through scholarships.

Learn More: www.naphill.org

Principle #7: Positive Mental Attitude –Interview with Lefford Fate

---

All things are possible for those who believe they are possible, you can if you think you can
~Napoleon Hill

Lefford, as we know, Napoleon Hill wrote about the Principle of a Positive Mental Attitude more than a couple of decades ago, so why is this relevant today?

Lefford Fate: I think it's relevant for today because there's so much negativity in the world today. If you pick up your paper, if you go on the Internet, if you watch television, Democrats, Republicans, Independents, Conservatives, Liberals, everybody's going at each other and it's negative, negative, negative. Let's be honest, if you wallow around in the mud, you're going to get dirty. So, if all you do is deal with negative, negative, negative, that's what's going to come out of your life and that's what's going to be a part of your life. I think in computer language they say it easily: garbage in, garbage out. So, I think it's very important that we pay attention to how we can be more positive. I'm not talking about being unrealistic but being positive in a way provides us hope. If we can do that, I think we'll be much better off.

We must remember to be realistic, so, how do you remain positive in things that are happening today that have negativity surrounding us?

Lefford Fate: Well, let's be honest, I hear that a lot when people are talking about realism and positivity. But, for every negative thing, there's a seed of an equivalent benefit. That was one of the precepts of Napoleon Hill. He said, if not for the fact that his mother had passed, and his father brought a new stepmother in, he would have probably been a newer, faster version of Jessie James. Bad things are going to happen in life. That's a fact. But you need to look at the situation and see what you can get out of that. That's the difference of something happening *to* you, and something happening *through* you. Because it's not our fault and it's not our responsibility what happens to us, just how we respond to that event. That is 100% our responsibility! It is up to us to work that process.

When you said, "to you" or "through you," this means reacting versus responding, right?

Lefford Fate: Right. The response is: What am I going to do with this? I'm going to stop and think. One of the blessings that we have is control of our own minds. We get to make the choice on how we're going to respond to what happens in our life.

That's just such a huge, huge point! So, there's to and through, there's reacting versus responding. Now, what do you feel some common misconceptions are about Positive Mental Attitude?

Lefford Fate: Sometimes, when people hear Positive Mental Attitude, they think of Pollyanna. They say things like, "Oh, they're naïve and they're not in touch with reality," but that's not the case. You can be positive about a situation, and still be totally engaged with reality. So, a lot of people think y'all are just walking around positive, positive, positive—they're suckers, they just don't know what's going on. But that's not the case. That's, again, a person taking their time and responding to the event and seeking that seed of an equivalent benefit. Now, when you say seed, that doesn't mean just think a positive thing, and everything just comes to light. What it means is, look for the seed, and then you need to nurture that seed to grow. That's what that means. So, there's a big old misconception that you either need to be positive or negative that there is no in between. You have to look for it, and you have to seek it. What you seek you shall find.

People may think, "Yay, Positive Mental Attitude makes everything go 'poof' and disappear." Have you noticed that?

Lefford Fate: Yes, and I think that's what sets people up for failure. Jim Rohn used to say, Some people decide to put their heads in the sand and say, "There are no weeds." If you believe that there are no weeds, the weeds will overtake the garden. So, you recognize and understand that there are negative things out there. However, if you know they're out there, you can combat them, you can prepare for them, this way you're responding versus reacting.

Let me use a personal example to demonstrate this. My mother-in-law passed recently. My wife had to go to the UK to help plan the funeral. She is struggling mightily. Now, some people would say, "What's the benefit of that?" Well, it's not a benefit, but what's going on is that she and her other siblings—who haven't always gotten along because, you know, trivial things get in the way—have had to come together and discuss the arrangement and just work through the process. It's bringing them closer together. I'm not saying that their mom's death is a good thing. They had to seek the seed of goodness. And all of them know that their mom would want the kids to get together and do well, to take care of their stepdad. That is a positive side out of that. Again, nobody would've wished for her death, but now there everyone has been given an opportunity to come together, love each other, and heal some wounds that have been placed there over the years.

The idea of a seed is so powerful about Positive Mental Attitude, you're not saying the other negative stuff goes away; you're just choosing to focus on the seed and fanning that ember so that does become a little bit better in the situation.

Lefford Fate: Yes, and it teaches many, many things that other members of the family or younger people need to understand—that this is a circle of life, and that these things happen. It also teaches you how to adjust and deal with other things, versus just saying "Woe is me" and catastrophizing the situation.

What positive changes did you experience in your life after applying this Principle to your personal and business life?

Lefford Fate: Yes. I remember when I was a young airman, we were at a club, dancing and hanging out, and somebody sucker-punched one of my friends. So, we all got into a fight. Now, it could've been just as easy to pull everybody out and go do something else and think about it and *not* get into a fight, but we started fighting. The negative part is that, months and months later, I was always looking to be mad at those certain people. It was a dumb thing—there was alcohol involved and people weren't doing the right thing—but we carried those negative feelings for a long time. It had some negative outcomes because it's hard to be a good airman when you're thinking negative thoughts and you're walking around with a chip on your shoulder.

Also, as a leader, there were times when I totally messed up. Sometimes, when you're a leader, other people may want to let things go, and you end up leading other people down the wrong path because the power of your personality. For me, as a leader, my biggest failures in my life is when I've led somebody else down the wrong path. Everything rises and falls on leadership, and you can lead somebody in the right direction or the wrong direction. And I hurt some people by leading them down the wrong path.

If you think about that one statement and if that domino starts falling in that direction, then that person is emulating what they saw from you. They start emulating it to their circle of influence and then it just becomes this domino effect in a negative way. But if you flip that and look at the opposite side—when you train and teach someone to choose and respond and not react and use that positive mental attitude—then look at that ripple effect or that domino effect, it becomes something that draws you into wanting to apply that positive mental attitude, because of the people around you.

Lefford Fate: Exactly! It's all about being positive and figuring out how to make the situation better, because, let's be honest, negative things and bad things are going to happen in this world. That is not negative thinking; that's truthful thinking. So, what are you going to do when it happens? Start thinking positive and looking for that seed of equivalent benefit! Then you can start nurturing that seed, and it will come out better on the other end. Look at diseases and the medicines that we have developed. Something negative happened, and then people found cures. That is that cycle: Something bad happens, somebody does something to fix it, and then we get better, we get stronger, we grow longer, and we live longer. It's basic science, basic common sense, if you think about it.

You're a Certified Napoleon Hill Leader. Being aware and noticing things in your own life is a big part of the battle. Can you think of a time when you've worked with someone and helped them notice an obstacle in their life and then apply this principle? How do you show and help the people you work with be aware, so that they can work through that with a Positive Mental Attitude?

Lefford Fate: There was a civil engineer I worked with, who had been working in his job for 23 years. This gentleman had become disenfranchised. He thought he was going to get a promotion, and he ended up not getting that promotion. So, he became disgruntled.

He went to his boss's boss and said, "Hey, if there's anything out there, such as a new position, I'd like to get it, because I'm not getting along with my boss."

Now, I don't think he meant to do what he did, but he basically "threw shade" or slammed his boss. So, the senior supervisor found a different place for him to go.

He wasn't happy with that position. Because he wasn't happy, his attitude was negative. So, he started kicking rocks and coming to work really frustrated with everything. Then he got to a point where he was going to be released or fired from his job because he was so negative all the time.

Then we started talking.

He came to me and I asked him, "How can this benefit you? What can you get out of this situation?"

Funny enough, he ended up deciding to retire. He was at a point in his life where he could retire from his job, he had done his time so to speak. He ended up taking what he was learning and had learned in current job and realized his talents. He said he started thinking "What can I do to do the job that I want?" He wasn't necessarily unhappy with the job; he was unhappy with his growth. Once he figured that out, he went out and made his own job!

Now he's a contractor and a consultant with his own company and he's really, really happy. That decision was based on taking at a look at what the benefit was and going through the process that he was going through. I think this was a huge win for him because he's now doing something that he really loves.

And he was too close to the situation at the moment to see all that. It took someone from the outside helping him to notice that.

Lefford Fate: Yeah. We do it a lot. There's an old story about the old hound dog that's sitting on the nail. He's just moaning and whining, and whining and moaning, and the owner of the dog said, "He's hurting but it doesn't hurt bad enough."

He was miserable and he wanted to do something different. He had caused some of his own issues, but then he stopped and thought about it, about "What is the benefit of me going through this?" Actually, he had to get a little bit more uncomfortable so he could get up and move to go to his happy place.

So, I think that was, to me, a great example, because I see that so often.

When I was in the military, I saw a lot of people get to their twenty years, and yet they didn't get out because they were afraid. They weren't happy until they were forced to get out or they were forced to say, "What can I do to make myself happy in this situation?"

What initially inspired you to become a Certified Leader through the Napoleon Hill Foundation?

Lefford Fate: Well, funny enough, I've been studying Napoleon Hill for years. One of my favorite supervisors, John Gunther, introduced me to reading and introduced me to Napoleon Hill. A couple years ago I did an interview with Steve Copeland, Steve has a close relationship with the Executive Director of the Napoleon Hill Foundation, so he introduced me to Mr. Don Green. After our interview Steve asked me a question I will never forget. He asked me what I wanted to do about my dream to help people suffering with Mental Health issues (especially veterans.

I said, "I want to do a *Think and Grow Rich* type of book for the military, because there are a lot of people in the military that do four years, or they do 20 years, or they do 30 years, and when they get out, they don't know what to do and where to go."

He told me that, "Napoleon Hill has an application process."

I figured that if I went through that process, it would get me closer to understanding all the principles. Then, based on that, as well as my 30 years of military service, I could help my military veterans do better and be better. Getting close to the Napoleon Hill Foundation would help me to be able to write that book, allowing me to be able to help my veterans.

I lost a really good friend because he did not see a way out. Instead, he self-medicated and basically drank himself to death because he could not get the help when he did that transition from military to civilian. If I can, I want to stop that from ever happening again. I also thought it would be a good way to be a great voice by me getting strong with all the principles of Napoleon Hill and putting that book together.

What is so great about your response is that part of your response was also about benefiting yourself as you look at improving other people's lives. Your approach is for a greater cause—not just for a friend or contact or military personnel. It's a whole movement!

There's a big difference between knowing and doing, or strategy and tactics. What do you think an implementation action plan is for Positive Mental Attitude?

Lefford Fate: I have a rule of five. I like to call this "The Fate Fab 5." I will tell anybody to do these things first.

One, when you get up in the morning, define the type of day that you want to have. Do this as soon as you wake up. Ask yourself, "What kind of a day am I going to have?" Then decide that it's going to be a good day.

Second, Success leaves clues, find a pacesetter, somebody you want to model yourself after, and follow that persons' direction towards a positive light. When I ran track, there was always a guy that was faster than me, and so I modeled myself after that guy.

Third, you're the average of the five people that you spend most time with. Charlie Tremendous Jones said that, and Jim Rohn said it, too. So, who are the five people closest to you in your life? Figure those five people out, and if you're the best in that group—the smartest, the brightest, the fastest—you might need to get another person or group in your life, so that you can be stronger, smarter, better, and faster.

Four is to implement what I like to call an "Hour of power." I take 20 minutes every day that I read, 20 minutes every day that I listen to some motivational messages, and 20 minutes a day that, as a minimum, I exercise. I do that in the morning, whether it's a little jog, pushups, jumping jacks, or whatever. So, do your hour of power every day. Read, listen, and exercise.

Finally, at the end of every day, write out what you're grateful for. I have a gratitude log that I write in before I go to sleep, and it has helped me to stay happy and positive. It's really hard to be negative when—especially, before you go to bed and you're starting to go into a dream state—you're thinking about all those positive things that go on in your life.

If you follow those 5 things, you will have a Positive Mental Attitude.

And just because of who I am, I want to throw an extra one in: Google 5 books about attitude and then read them. If you want to be wealthy, study wealth. If you want to be physically fit, study physical fitness. If you want to have a great positive attitude, study Positive Mental Attitude. These are my keys or my steps to success.

Finally—even if you don't know me from a can of paint, guys—take care of our veterans. You got people that are standing in the gap for our freedom, every day, and if you could do that, you would honor me.

There's a quote, it's by a guy named Dr. William James, and it's amazing. It says, "The greatest discovery of my generation is that human beings can alter their lives by altering their attitudes." I love that quote because it basically says that we determine our outcome based on how we think about our own attitudes.

You have met your Fate; let's walk into your destiny.

About Lefford Fate

Professionally I've led, mentored, and served thousands of military members and their families during my 30 years in the United States Air Force.

Since retiring from the military, I have been the program director for the geriatric outpatient mental health program, deputy Director for Health Services, SC Department of Corrections,

and now the Director Support Services, City of Sumter.

I am a husband, father, and grandfather, so I know it is not always easy to juggle our list of daily responsibilities. This makes it even more important to have a structured, practical plan in place to avoid becoming overwhelmed. I hold a Master's Degree in Human Relations and a Bachelor's Degree in Social Psychology. Modeling the core values of Integrity first, Service before self and Excellence in all I do.

I believe there is a "why" for everyone; that each of us was created with the potential to achieve greatness, to make a difference

in the world, to add value to others, and as a result, experience a full and rewarding life. For over 30 years, my purpose was to defend our nation, and now that purpose is helping people discover their life's purpose and grow to their full potential.

Learn More: http://www.leffordfate.com

Principle #8: Enthusiasm – Interview with Lefford Fate

Enthusiasm is more powerful than logic, reason, or rhetoric in getting your ideas across and in winning over others, to be enthusiastic we must act enthusiastically
~Napoleon Hill

Lefford, what makes the Principle of Enthusiasm relevant for today?

Lefford Fate: What makes it relevant today, for me, is that we have to really want to do what we say we want to do. So many people are doing things because their parents want them to do it, because their friends want them to do it, because their spouses want them to do it, or because that's what society says you want to do, so when you do things that way, you're only doing them "kind of." But when you're enthusiastic about something, you're doing it because you want it. It's your heart's blood and it matters to you. When it matters to you and you put Enthusiasm behind your Definite Major Purpose, then you can get it done. We need people that are passionate about what they do.

If you were to ask social psychologists today what the biggest influences on society are, I feel like misdirection and things like stress would be some of the prevalent answers. So, do you feel like Enthusiasm, aligned with Definite Major Purpose, really helps to combat some of those?

Lefford Fate: I do. I'm a person of faith so, to me, Enthusiasm comes from within. It's God within you—the energy and inspiration within you—trying to get out.

I honestly think that we'd have a lot fewer problems and issues in the world if people were more enthusiastic about what they wanted or needed to do. If you're not sure that you're doing the right thing—if you're not happy about what you're doing, if you're just doing it because somebody's dragging it out of you— it's hard to be enthusiastic and put your best foot forward. I believe that one thing that would make a person better off is if they would get behind something that they really want and play all out toward their definite goal.

What misconceptions are out there surrounding Enthusiasm?

Lefford Fate: I actually think there are a several misconceptions out there. One is thinking that you have to feel a certain way before you can get things done. Some think it is automatic for them to wake up motivated. Almost like, you wake up and say, "I don't feel like it." I think that you have to act your way into feeling, instead of waiting for the feelings to show up.

To be enthusiastic, you act enthusiastic. To be happy, you act happy. It's putting yourself in that state. I'm a TEDx speaker, and one of my favorite TED Talks' speakers is Amy Cuddy. She does the Wonder Woman pose. You can act your way into something before you really feel it. So, I think that's a huge misconception— that you have to wait to feel good to do good.

Do you know about the actual physiological effects that go on in your mind and body, when you are in confident pose?

Lefford Fate: Yes. When you do the confident pose, your physical state determines your body. We are a mind and body connected. We're not just a body. We're a body with a spirit, and we're gifted with intellect. So, when you change your physical state, you can change your emotional state. When you change your physical state, you can change your intellectual state.

There were studies done where a person put a pencil in their teeth, which causes a smile action, versus where you put a pencil in your lips, which causes a frown action. You behave and feel differently just by changing one particular state. So, I think you can act in the way that you want to be. You simply force your way. I call it a "Mind Hack".

I've done a lot of mind hacks in my life. One is where I wake up and say, "I'm going to be happy and enjoy today!" Because I make a public declaration and I'm enthusiastic about it, my day is a better day! It's not like, "Woe is me." It's like, "Whoa! I get to do this!"

Do you feel like people that are not as familiar with these types of mind hacks and affirmations, need to make their statements detailed, or can they simply say, "I'm going to have a wonderful day"?

Lefford Fate: I hear it all the time and I see people do that. It's a feeling. It doesn't have to be perfect. Jim Rohn used to say, "Some people get so caught up in studying the root that they don't pick the fruit." There are times to study the roots, but if I can say it with my Georgia slang and I feel really good about it, I'm going to go with that, versus saying it perfectly just so it's clean for somebody else. Bottom line, I believe we can affirm our desires and go for it as best we can. As Maya Angelou stated "when we know better, we can do better" do it the best you can and then we work on improving it. I believe we start where we are, or desires, and that works better than saying it perfectly and not doing anything towards your desired goal.

Since we're talking about misconceptions, people may feel like Enthusiasm is viewed as "Rah! Rah!" pep rally excited. Is that something you hear from time to time? People saying, "I'm just not that kind of person." Well, maybe that's not what you need to be.

Lefford Fate: Yes, I hear that. It's like the twin sister of the other misconception.

Another misconception I think, is that you can be "Rah! Rah!" in your positive affirmation and not put in the work, because faith without work is dead. So, if you're enthusiastic, you put action behind that enthusiasm. You can be unenthusiastic, if you want, and just sit on your bum and not go do anything, but if you do that, nothing is going to grow.

It is Enthusiasm with a Definite Major Purpose and taking definite action for something that you want to do with a burning desire that is the formula to success.

It's kind of like saying "Knowledge is Power" is a nice phrase that sounds good, but it's really not the truth. Knowledge is potential power, but you must do something behind it.

Lefford Fate: Right, and I think that's the misconception that many of us find. It's not an "Either/or." It's a "Yes/and."

If you're enthusiastic and then you go do something about it, that will just lead to more Enthusiasm. It's a momentum thing, like if you think positively and then you do positive acts, it makes you feel more positive. Then you think you can, and then you go do more. Then you see the results and then you start doing more, and then you start seeing other results. It's like an upward spiral, because you're actually doing something with those thoughts and feelings and behaviors.

That's what I think is the win.

You see that all the time in leadership and management. For example, say you saw one of your subordinates doing something wrong. You could just blast them, or you could watch for ways they're doing something right, then guide them and encourage them and give them praise for that, so that you get more of that, and then just give them a nice, little gentle nudge for the wrong thing.

If you do that, then that person will see a little bit of good as well as your implementation towards the Positive Mental Attitude, Major Purpose, with Enthusiasm. Then both of you will feel like, "You know, that kind of worked pretty good here. I feel good about that," and you'll want to do more. Because we always want to do more of stuff that makes us feel good.

Lefford Fate: Exactly. That's one of the things that I talk about all the time with raising children and developing employees as a leader. If you reward people for the good things they do, they will do great things, you get whatever you reward them for.

So, praise them for whatever you want them to do more of.

I always tell the story about when my wife and I first started dating. I had this gray shirt with a little small white collar, and I remember she walked up to me and she rubbed across my shoulder, and she was like, "I really like that shirt." I went out and bought ten other shirts just like it. They're just different colors. She changed my behavior based on her response to something I wore, and I wanted to keep getting that reaction. Let's just say, I was quite enthusiastic about impressing my wife with the way I dressed.

So, it's true. You reward a behavior and that behavior will be repeated for you.

What positive changes did you experience in your life after applying this Principle to your personal and business life?

Lefford Fate: Well, it's really funny. I was a very successful military man. I retired as the Command Chief of the 20th Fighter Wing, the premier F16 Aircraft Wing in the world. I was in the top 1% of the top 1%, as the Command Chief. That's the distinction. But when I got out of the military, I didn't "speak civilian." I was really nervous about that transition. It was a little rough. So, I went to Toastmasters to learn how to speak civilian. Initially, when I started out, I was a little bit awkward and nervous, because I didn't speak like normal people in the civilian sector spoke. So, what I found myself doing was doing it afraid speaking tentatively but doing it anyway. Then I started to get better. I started speaking. Then I started training. Then I started coaching. As I started to gain more momentum, as I did more of it, I felt better about myself. A couple of people would say, "You're pretty good," or "If you did this, you'd get better." So, I listened, and the more I did it, the better I got. The better I got, the more enthusiasm and passion I had. It resonated with people and I connected with more people, and then I started to grow.

Now, I have a full-time position with the city of Sumter, South Carolina, but I am also a speaker, trainer, and coach. I travel around the U.S., and I'm going to Sweden this year, to speak at an event there. So, it was just being enthusiastic, learning, studying, and as I grew, the momentum built. Then I felt better and I do better now. Enthusiasm changed my life and outlook, in the area of professional and public speaking.

One thing that stands out in what you just said was you wanted to achieve that next level of speaking civilian, but you didn't try to Google it and try to find it out on your own. You went to some organization—in your case, Toastmasters—that had a proven plan to help you.

Lefford Fate: Exactly, and one of the things that happens (as I've said before) is that success leaves clues. When I went to

Toastmasters, they introduced me to other leaders, other speakers, and other trainers. Then they introduced me to more. You don't always have to know the end or your destination; sometimes, you just have to take that next step, and that'll lead you to the next step, and that'll lead you to the next step. So, you're starting the process. If you keep moving and keep looking for growth, there are a lot of opportunities out there.

As a Napoleon Hill Certified Leader, I know you work with clients. Can you think of some example of how you worked with someone who is now experiencing some of the benefits of implementing Enthusiasm into their day? What did you do with them to help them get to where they are now?

Lefford Fate: I won't go into great detail, but will say a name, Dom Faussette. He was an Airman, and he was a policeman. When he wanted to get into professional speaking, a Chief Master Sergeant friend of mine introduced us, and we got together and started talking on the phone. I coached Dom into going out and becoming a speaker and going to Toastmasters and joining the John Maxwell team. I taught him to be more enthusiastic about what he can actually do, and not worry about what the naysayers said. I helped him focus on what he really wanted to do. I asked him, "What's your Definite Major Purpose? Decide that and go get what you want."

To me, Dom was good anyway, before speaking to me, but I call him my success story, because he actually left his corporate job, wrote a book, and became a professional speaker. He's traveling around the world, speaking, now. And that's strictly because he decided that he was going to do it and he put a burning desire behind that decision.

You probably guided him into some of these things and showed him what could be a reality. It was always in him and it came out, because he had that focus and unleashed it. We've got stuff inside of us that we don't even know, until we start taking that first step and that next step, and then the next step after that.

Lefford Fate: Exactly. That's why I say coaching is so very, very important. I am who I am now because of mentors, coaches, and leaders in my life, because even when I didn't think I could do it, somebody else was there, thinking I could. That's why I like to say I do mind hacks. Sometimes, I have to believe in myself when other people don't believe in me and other times, I surround myself with people who think highly of me when I don't think highly of myself, and they encourage me.

What's an implementation or an action plan for Enthusiasm?

Lefford Fate: The first thing to do is to adopt a Major Definite Purpose for your life. What is it that you want to do? What is your dream? I tell people all the time that it doesn't matter how fantastical your dream is. Dream! Because most people—and this is accredited to Les Brown—don't miss in life because they aim too high. They aim too low and they hit. And many people don't even aim at all.

The next thing is to back that Purpose with a burning desire and stoke that fire. You want it, but you have to make that a white-hot heat. Read books, read magazines, and listen to motivational things so you can keep stoking that fire!

The third thing is to write your Purpose out. Put it in front of you. Put it on your computer screen, put is on your phone, put it on your mirror. I have affirmations in my phone and on my desktop, so I have stuff that keeps coming out all the time that says, "Hey, be the best speaker in South Carolina. Be a good husband. Be a good father." I also write it out and I keep that stuff in front of me. I repeat and memorize the things that I want to get in my life.

One of the hacks that I do is this: I tell people what I'm going to do. I have some friends who, if you tell them what you're going to do and you don't do it, they are going to come at you until you do it. So, the fourth thing to do is to find that person who you can tell your goals and desires that that will hold you accountable.

Five is to stay away from negative people. It's hard, but if you hang around with one negative person, and you tell that person what you want to do they will pull you down—tell you that you can't do it, or that you'll never survive—it's going to hurt your chances of being successful.

You asked for five, but I always give an extra. The sixth one is to find yourself a cheerleader. Who is that person that's got your back, who will tell you, "You can do it!"? Find that person. And the best way to find that person is to be that person for somebody else.

About Lefford Fate

Professionally I've led, mentored, and served thousands of military members and their families during my 30 years in the United States Air Force.

Since retiring from the military, I have been the program director for the geriatric outpatient mental health program, deputy Director for Health Services, SC Department of Corrections,

and now the Director Support Services, City of Sumter.

I am a husband, father, and grandfather, so I know it is not always easy to juggle our list of daily responsibilities. This makes it even more important to have a structured, practical plan in place to avoid becoming overwhelmed. I hold a Master's Degree in Human Relations and a Bachelor's Degree in Social Psychology. Modeling the core values of Integrity first, Service before self and Excellence in all I do.

I believe there is a "why" for everyone; that each of us was created with the potential to achieve greatness, to make a difference

in the world, to add value to others, and as a result, experience a full and rewarding life. For over 30 years, my purpose was to defend our nation, and now that purpose is helping people discover their life's purpose and grow to their full potential.

Learn More: http://www.leffordfate.com

Principle #9: Self-Discipline – Interview with John Raniola

---

*The great master key to riches is nothing more or
less than the self-discipline necessary to help you
take full and complete possession of your own mind*
~Napoleon Hill

John, why is the Principle of Self-Discipline relevant for today?

John Raniola: To me, Self-Discipline—as Napoleon Hill
touches on it—is to control your mind, your thoughts, and your
actions. If you cannot control your actions, your mind, or your
thoughts, you're not going to be able to control your reality, how
you vision life and everything else, or your perspective in life.

How does being self-aware tie into that?

John Raniola: When you have something negative going on, you
start realizing your life is spiraling out of control. This happens
for many people and they're not even witnessing that their lives
are being lived out. Once you know how to control your mind or
your thoughts, and you're disciplined in that, you're able to shut
down those negative thoughts and shift your thoughts and your
actions towards your goals, to be a happier person and change the
circumstances.

A lot of people will get into this negative spiral, where everything
just spins out of control and things just get worse and worse. If
you're able to train your mind to understand that this is happening
to you and able to shift your focus, you can get yourself out of
most negative situations.

Today, people are so overloaded with busyness, technology, and really overwhelming themselves, how would you advise people to be present and watch their attitudes, so that they can start applying Self-Discipline?

John Raniola: First, I want to touch on something. Napoleon Hill's philosophy is not just about society and the things that are around us and our business. It's about life, it's about the mind. It's about the law of life and success and how one lives their life. Even though his philosophy from the 1920s to now is somewhat the same, society has changed a little, so we must adapt a little.

I have found that we have 24-hour news on every day, which is just feeding people negativity, anger, and hate. Very rarely, you'll see something positive on the news. People are watching this day in and day out, for hours straight. They wake up in the morning and they listen to this and they can't even—and I believe it's a fear that they don't want to—listen to themselves. They don't want to face themselves, so they must listen to noise, which blocks you out from yourself. You're forming a mindset through that, watching that news and all that negative stuff.

To top it off, I walked in the gym today, this morning, and everywhere I went, the news was on every wall. Every time I turned to the left or right, looked up, or went on the treadmill, there was a TV with the news on—on every single piece of equipment. So, people aren't even shutting down at the gym anymore. They're somewhat being programmed by the media, by the news.

On top of the news, all you're watching is medication commercials—one medication commercial after another. When you start understanding how powerful the mind is, you understand that whatever it is that you hear often, you start believing. So, when you start repeating this medication commercial—oh, you have this, and you have this, do you have that?—some people, I believe, are actually creating a lot of these illnesses through their minds. So, this is developing people to get illnesses and it's just treating the symptom and not the source.

If you have Self-Discipline in your habits and your patterns of life, you can change a lot of illnesses because many of the illnesses are caused by your habits, your thought patterns, and everything else. We are really making ourselves mentally ill. And by being mentally ill, we are also becoming physically ill.

What misconceptions are out there surrounding the Principle of Self-Discipline?

John Raniola: When I was growing up, before I got into this philosophy, I thought discipline meant I had to work really hard, punish myself, and really do things to the extreme. But once you start learning how to control your Self-Discipline, you start realizing that the real thing that is controlling people is the fight within. So, the most strenuous conflict than anyone will face will be the one from within. And if they lack Self-Discipline, they will never, ever be able to overcome the person within that is holding them back. I believe that that's the biggest misconception—that we think we have to work hard.

We must get Self-Discipline over our minds, how we talk to each other, and how we act.

And then that carries over into other areas of our life, right?

John Raniola: Yes, because once you start Self-Discipline in your mind and can start focusing, you could get to where everything just starts to fall into place. You end up becoming a better person, a better man.

What positive changes did you experience in your life after applying this Principle to your personal and business life?

John Raniola: I was born into and brought up with a very negative outlook on life. I had parents who believed that everyone was already successful. No one could become successful anymore. And I was talked out of going after my dreams and things like that. I had to do this myself, so one thing was getting the strength and the power to be alone on my journey, going towards my dreams, or figuring out what my dreams were. Another positive was overcoming my fears and my personality. I changed my whole life and everything about my life—physically and mentally—inside and out.

I transformed from a negative mental attitude into a Positive Mental Attitude. This wasn't simple; it took years and years of fighting. Like I said before, we fight ourselves. I could have been a lot more ahead, but I fight myself. I fight the old me, who wants to come back, which I talk a lot about, regarding past generations and things like that.

So, Self-Discipline doesn't only overcome your negativity, your anger, or your way of looking at life—because your parents' generation created that into you. You're actually going back there and disciplining your ancestors. You're changing the whole outlook of your whole family for the future. I transformed my past generation's belief system. I Self-Disciplined myself to overcome the fear to quit my job and to do something totally new, which was outrageous.

Can you share an example of how you have helped a client overcome these obstacles and succeed in using Self-Discipline in their personal or business life?

John Raniola: Yes. I teach a way of silencing the mind, where you shut off negative thoughts and reverse them into something positive. When I teach people that, they start getting Self-Discipline of their thoughts. Most people are going around with their thoughts running themselves and most of them are negative.

And if we don't know how to control them, they could run for days without us even having focused on that. So, we need to learn how to stop it. One of the first lessons I try to teach is to learn how to shut down.

I received this one day. I had put a comment up on Facebook. I didn't think anything of it, and it changed someone's life. Just one simple comment. This person came to me and said that they were really having deep, deep issues. They said that my post actually changed their perspective and they changed their whole lives. I watch them grow, on Facebook, and I'm really impressed how they changed their life over one quote.

So, there is a lot you can change. Self-Discipline is changing your whole lifestyle, your whole world, everything around you, your surroundings. When you start disciplining everything, you start changing your attraction and then that attraction returns to you. So, what's happening is, by teaching others to control their thoughts or to shut down a negative, they're finding that they no longer fit in that negative surrounding anymore. They grow out of that negative surrounding and they do not want to be around those people anymore because they're starting to drain them.

I learned that years ago, on my journey, because all I knew was negative. I didn't know anyone positive. I didn't know anyone successful. This was something all new to me. Even on my journey, I watched people that I believed were successful find out they weren't successful, especially in the mind.

Do you find that when people start taking baby steps and seeing some slight improvement, that it motivates them to take that next step?

John Raniola: Yes. A lot of people believe that success is going to come overnight, that there's a magic tool, or some kind of magic potion, or some secret. The thing is, you have to do this in little steps. You're transforming generations and generations of thought patterns, and it's not going to happen overnight. It's going to happen in little, baby steps, because you have to, little by little, travel towards a better you.

I believe a lot of people get lost focusing on the big tools to success that a lot of people are selling out there. And people just sit back and go, "Okay, let's do the simplest tool possible." Because I tell people, when they're looking to do something, I ask them, what's the simplest tool that they could use? There was a lady that wanted to open a business. I'm not going to go into details, but I asked her, "What is the simplest thing to do?"

And she said, "I don't know, I need a website."

I'm like, "Okay, so tonight go out on the Internet and get dot-com name. I don't care if it's right or wrong, just get a dot-com name."

She asked, "What is that going to do?"

I reply, "You just got rid of Step One. Now you can concentrate on Step Two, and as you're going down your steps, if you want to change your dot-com name, who cares? It's only a few dollars to buy dot-com name. But to take that step and get your focus out of Step One and then start focusing it on Step Two, Step Three, I will tell you, when you start taking the small steps, they will start taking a life of their own. They will start getting bigger and bigger and bigger and bigger. Then, you'll want to challenge yourself more and more, because you're going to see what you're becoming. You're becoming something powerful, your energy is rising, and you're just growing faster and faster and faster. Once you tap into this, you are not going to want to be around the old you anymore. You're going to want to learn, get as much knowledge as possible, and get out there and grow. As Napoleon Hill put it, you will 'Think and grow rich.'"

What inspired you to become a Napoleon Hill Certified Leader and what words of encouragement would you give to others considering becoming one as well?

John Raniola: Tell you the truth, I wasn't looking to be certified. I was seeking knowledge; I was seeking wisdom. There was something in Napoleon Hill's writing that was guiding me back to Napoleon Hill. One night, I sat at the computer and I was confused about my journey. I got stuck and asked, "What am I missing? What am I missing?"

So, I started researching Napoleon Hill's self-development books and I came across the Napoleon Hill Foundation. I went on there and I looked at it and I said, "You know what? I am going to do this. This sounds challenging. I want to do this."

This was not the easiest thing for me. I had to overcome a lot.

I did not like to read. I did not like to study, and I was never good at school. I had to sit down and take these courses, which was amazing, because it taught me Self-Discipline. It taught me about this, and it reshaped my mind.

The next day, I looked on the website, and I called Don Green, the CEO of the Napoleon Hill Foundation. When I talked to him, I didn't even know he was a CEO. Talking to him made me feel like I was one with him, and it wasn't like I was scared that this was a big CEO or anything like that. When I talked to him, we went mind to mind, and it was an amazing thing. I think that drove me, too, because I realized that there was something there that I was missing, that I had to find. And just that mind to mind, where you can have a positive conversation with someone, was amazing to me, and that's what really drew me into the certificate.

Now, going after this, doing all this studying, and getting certified opened my world to a totally different thing because I didn't do this to teach others, to guide others. I did this to guide myself to become a better person. It just so happened that I could see what's holding people down. So, I know now how I can teach them to get out of that lifestyle, that situation.

That's where, if you want to really dig deep into this philosophy, I would totally recommend anyone to take the certificate and then go out there, meet the Napoleon Hill Foundation in Virginia or wherever they're having their classes, and see what kind of people they are. Because I am telling you right now, these people want you to think for yourself and want you to create your dreams, your passions, and they're not going to force things onto you—like I believe a lot of other people out there would do. This is a real, genuine foundation and I'm really ecstatic and really happy to be a part of it.

What do you think an implementation action plan is for the Principle of Self-Discipline?

John Raniola: Like I said before, it's the baby steps. These are the things that people are missing and these are the things that are going to transform your life the best. These are the steps that I had to do, and these are the steps I teach people. I know that they're going to say it's silly and whatnot, but this is very powerful, and it really needs to become very disciplined and become a ritual.

Number One, you have to smile more and be overly polite. So, when you're going through a doorway, you smile. You say, "Thank you." You say, "You're welcome." You just be very overly polite, and you will see that you will shock people. People will be like, "Whoa, what's going on here?" Because they're not used to seeing this. But I will tell you, as you start changing your smile, just a simple smile and being over-polite, you are going to start changing your world. You'll start to shift your world. You're going to start seeing more and more positive people going past you, in that doorway, and you're not going to get that negative person that's angry. I don't know how; it's like it is like magic, like the negative people fade away.

Another thing is to learn to accept a "thank you." There are a lot of people out there, helping people out, doing good, and things like that. They would say, "Thank you." But I would say, "No, no, no, no. Thank *you*." You must learn how to accept saying,

"You're welcome," because that is everything in life—you must accept it. Really, if we look deep into it, we, a lot of people, are accepting negative or we're accepting positive. So, accepting a "thank you" starts to develop you to accepting things, and you start changing your energy.

The next thing is to change the words you speak. Stop cursing. Cursing is a negative energy and draws negative people to you. You also need to change the words that you say to yourself.

A test I do to everyone, so I know exactly where they are is that I ask them, "How are you?" When their answer comes back, "I'm fine," or they want to tell me their whole life story or that everything's falling apart, I know that these people are people I don't want to be around. But you notice they're on their journey if someone says, "Oh, I'm great! I'm doing phenomenal, I'm doing fantastic!" They are not negative anymore, they're positive—even if they're faking it, in the beginning, because you have to fake it in the beginning.

The other thing that you have to make sure of is that you say, "I am phenomenal." Do not feel bad about making other people feel bad because they're not doing so great or they're not happy with life. You must let that go, because this is developing the Self-Discipline and the power and your energy within. So, you have to go out there and say you're doing great, say you're doing phenomenal, and just let the negative people go. Let them fade away.

The next one is to create an affirmation. This is learning what to say to yourself, and this is a very powerful thing. This is the "I am…" Everything after I am, I become. So, you must make this very powerful. It has to be "I am" as the moment, as of now. So, "I am wealthy, I am a millionaire, I am healthy. I am this." I made this mistake in the beginning, where I used my affirmation as, "I am going to be, I am going to be…" You cannot do that. It has to be "I am now…" because we are disciplining our minds to create this world for us.

This philosophy is very powerful and when you get Self-Discipline, your mind and your world just really spirals into a positive one.

The next one is to have a Definite Major Purpose. If people do not have a Definite Major Purpose, they are confused. They don't know what their purpose is. They are living other people's ideas, other people's thoughts. So, do not worry about it, just make yourself, your Definite Major Purpose. Start with little steps, but you must write it down. You must write down your Definite Major Purpose and you must read it every morning, every night, as a ritual. It has to become a ritual. You have to read it every morning, every night. This is training your subconscious mind to start thinking more positive and to start working for your purpose. Your mind is very powerful, and it will show you the way. It's you that must get out of its way. You must get yourself there, and your mind will show you the way. This is the beginning of telling your mind what you want and what you want to develop in life.

This is very important, too. Put this, your Definite Major Purpose, on a piece of paper, and hang it on the wall. Hang it up in the bathroom, if you have to, even if you have to put a little clip on the shower door so you can read it while you're taking a shower. Put it everywhere you can see it, so your subconscious mind and your mind starts to develop it.

About John Raniola

My journey started in the year 2013, I hit rock bottom, and I believe that my mind triggered into survival mode, I lived my life with crippling fears about everything, I was angry, out of shape and disliked myself, I was miserable drinking at night, and I was spending 4-6 hours a day sitting in bumper to bumper traffic. My life had spired out of control. One day I started to listen to motivational videos on my phone in traffic which reminded me that years before I had bought an audiobook that I began to listen to, I thought at the time I was being foolish and threw that audiobook in a drawer.

I was finally ready for growing my life out of the negative lifestyle that I was born into, into a more successful outlook in life. I was finally prepared to do something with my life. The audiobook in the drawer was, "Think and Grow Rich" Gold Standard Collector's Edition by Napoleon Hill. I listened to the entire audiobook. My mind was blown wide opened.

Shortly after that and with many repeated listening, I finally found the courage to open a business and quit my job. I have created Raniola Mechanical & Maintenance Corp. an Air-conditioning and heating company on Long Island New York. Becoming a business owner alone taught me enormously about other people's habits and patterns and guided me not to copy their actions and to develop my own patterns. Most importantly becoming a business owner with the support of great writings like Think and Grow rich guided me through my fears.

If you remove all your fears, all that you will have left is "success."

During this time, I was writing notes, and writing down any information that revealed itself to me, and I started to write a book. I felt I had to. The writing was not easy for me, for I never liked to write, read or study. I am now an author of the book "Self-heal and become success." My life and business journey, reading self-improvement books. I had to travel alone on my journey for my old surroundings and yes including family would have talked me out of my passions, and I was not disciplined enough not to listen to them.

Behind your most significant fears hide your greatest assets.

I was so fascinated with my development, and I found something in Napoleon Hills writing, that kept me returning to his work, there was something I did not find in any other books or from today's motivators. Something was drawing me towards the Napoleon Hill Foundation, and that was to find my purpose. My purpose was giving to me as a project, "Self-discipline." Self-discipline was what I was missing in my life. I lacked discipline, or at least I needed to focus more on disciplining my thoughts, beliefs, emotional and action patterns that I was choosing in life. Are your habits controlling you or are you managing your patterns? We are our habits, let those habits be very disciplined towards our Definite Major Purpose.

It took me years to recognize this; we do not read the books we develop, Heal, grow and discipline ourselves into understanding the books through our journey creating our purpose into reality.

Believe me when I tell you. I used, reading self-development books and using mind manifesting tools as an excuse that I was not ready to "take action" in reality. I have spent an abundant of my time and money hiding behind fears. I have found this to be a significant issue all around the world causing people to give up on life development books and their dreams.

I decided to build a website with writings that I believe can help people understand Self- development books just a little faster than it took me. I am working on adding, tools, training and online classes on this website soon.

The one thing that I have recognized, I was returning to myself, my dreams, my ideas. Returning2Success.com. I ask this whose dreams are we chasing? Whose definition of success are we becoming? Return to your purpose for you and your journey hold all the secrets to success. I found myself and others focused on seeking a secret to success causing myself and many to lose precious time or to give up on their dreams.

I created Self-heal and become Success Corp. "Elite life Patterns Coaching." Self-healing one's past while they transform their future.

If you believe success is a secret that only the rich know, you will always be seeking a secret.

Learn More: www.returning2success.com

Principle #10: Accurate Thinking – Interview with Johnnie Lloyd

---

Whatever the mind can conceive and believe,
the mind can achieve.
~Napoleon Hill

Johnnie, what is the Principle of Accurate Thinking and why is it relevant for today?

Johnnie Lloyd: I call Accurate thinking the three pounds of unlimited power. Since it is the power of thought, it can be both positive and negative, both dangerous and innovative, and both beneficial and destructive. Accurate thinking is power to take control of our own mind.

We get so much information from media, Google, and other places, but we don't necessarily accurately deal with the information, it is important how we process because information is just data. Now, the relevance is that we need to be able to take that information and use deductive and inductive reasoning to determine "What is opinion and what is fact?" Then we need to separate those facts in our head, or even in our lives, as "What's fiction, what's hearsay, and what can be supported by evidence?" If we're not able to do that, it becomes very painful to have all that information and no way to dissect it.

If we broke it down into small segments, every single one of those would make total sense. But that sounds like a lot of work.

Johnnie Lloyd: It is.

So, how do you advise someone that would hear that and say, "I agree I do need to have Accurate Thinking, but, wow, all those steps at a moment's notice throughout the day, every day, all the time? That's a lot of work!" How do you address that?

Johnnie Lloyd: It's really addressed by looking at the result, not just the work. If we look at it from being result-oriented, we'll go through the work, because it costs us money, time, and our health if we go in the wrong direction, or to gain information that is not accurate, and we make decisions based on that.

But we also have common sense. Some of these things thrown our way just don't make sense. You can also look at them and ask, "Are they trying to entice me? Are they trying to influence me? Do they really want my money?" This is a quick check you can do that you can turn into a habit. As you build that habit, it doesn't take that much work.

That's a big one, too, because you might break down those points of pausing, reflecting, and thinking accurately, right? So, even if you know there are four, five, or six steps, but you just work on the first one and make that a habit, it then becomes like a needle in a record where you know it's in the groove, and you're not going to get out of it. Then you can work on the next piece of it.

Johnnie Lloyd: That's the other thing: look at your life. Is this not working for you? Maybe it may be great information, but it may not be accurate for you, so make it personal.

Is it true that Accurate Thinking can be right for one person and be different but still right for another person? How does Accurate Thinking remain the same as well as change, from person to person?

Johnnie Lloyd: Okay, so there's a couple of things. Truth is truth. For example, gravity is a principle. It's just true. It's not based on your opinion, it's just true. Then you have some situations where someone says, "I did this for (or with) my child" but who doesn't have children and is trying to give you information. Well, they don't have the basis. That person doesn't have the basis to accurately give you information as to how you should work with your child. And even if it did work for their child, it doesn't mean it will work for yours. All of us have heredity and social influence, so what works for one person doesn't necessarily work for another. You have to work what works for you.

Now, again, truth is truth and a lie is a lie, so we must look at it from that perspective, too. But we must make it personal and see how we're going to grow from that.

That's a big point, because the environment you are in or have been brought up in would change that scenario. Someone living in a small town might say, "Using Accurate Thinking, I want to give you some advice: You need to go work for the factory to succeed." Well, for that person in that small town, the only employer is the factory, but you can't put that out there for every human being, because someone else might live in New York City and say, "What's a factory?" Truth is truth, but then there's the application of your personal environment, upbringing, and sociological perspective, and all of that that needs to be layered in. That's a really good insight.

What is something else that would be a misconception about Accurate Thinking?

Johnnie Lloyd: One of the misconceptions is that the computer or all the technology takes the place of Accurate Thinking. With all the information out there, we need to think even more accurately.

One of the things that Napoleon Hill brings up is one of the most powerful thought processes of the benefits of Accurate Thinking. When you don't think accurately, it impacts every aspect of your life negatively, but when you think accurately, you think from a perspective of self-awareness.

That's the other thing. For some people, the misconception is, "I don't need to be aware of myself, of who I am, or what I was created to do." But that purpose leads to your accurate thought as to what your future is, where you direct your resources, and where you direct your energy. A huge misconception is that we do not have to control our lives. However, the truth is, if we don't control our lives, somebody else is in control.

Here's a deeper thought on that: If you don't control your life, someone else is in control, and guess who gave them that control? You did, by default.

Johnnie Lloyd: Exactly, by default. That's right. You know. But some people don't get it.

A simple analogy for me that I use, sometimes, when I train, is a ship with the rudder. The rudder is a small thing attached to the ship, but it helps give it direction and focus. That's the way our brain is. Our brain and Accurate Thinking will take us in the direction we need to go, with the focus we need. It also tweaks things. If we made a bad decision today or it wasn't the best decision, we learn from that and we build on that and, hopefully, make better decisions in the future.

But like you said, if we don't control ourselves, someone else will take control, and we gave them that. We don't want to be victims. We want to be victorious, so we need that control.

Eleanor Roosevelt was known for saying, "No one can make you feel inferior without your consent." Meaning it's you; it's all you, and that's a big a-ha—you lose control by not taking control. You're giving it away, but the action started with you, and it wasn't an aggressive or offensive action, it was the action of inaction.

I'm confident that Accurate Thinking is something someone could develop over time, what positive changes did you experience in your life after applying this Principle to your personal and business life?

Johnnie Lloyd: I like that question because I haven't always been where I am right now.

One of the things that happened in my life is as an executive—and coming from a place of homelessness in the past and building up—is that I started taking control of areas in my life. Accurate Thinking then caused me to steer other people instead of trying to control them. I was then able to help them, give them information, and give them instructions so they can make their own decisions. That's what happened in my life. I ended up thinking differently and, because my thought process happened differently, I was able to start serving people instead of attempting to control them.

That sounds like what they say in martial arts: Don't try to stop the punch, just kind of divert it so that it takes their energy and it moves it in another direction. You don't absorb it.

Johnnie Lloyd: Right, because now I'm happier because I think better. It's what Napoleon Hill meant when he said, "Whatever the mind can conceive and believe, it can achieve." The words here that are critical is "can achieve." It doesn't mean because I think it, I can have it. I have the capacity to achieve it. Now, my life is happier, I'm healthier, and I give more to other people.

I help people think critically, because that's the key, even if children don't even understand at the time. I gave my daughter a decision to make, in the confines of great decisions—the three decisions were good for me, regardless of the one she chose. However, I let her start thinking things out and making decisions and learning. That's what we sometimes miss today—the power that comes from building the muscle in the mind to accurately think.

That's huge, because that muscle is built through repetition. Then, when the next opportunity comes to use that Accurate Thinking muscle, it's easier because you've already conditioned it that way. It becomes a natural reflex. It's not work, it's not hard, it's just how now you operate.

Johnnie Lloyd: Right, because life is not perfect. We have to work through the imperfections to get to perfection so we're in a place of harmony and we're doing what we're passionate about.

I have a quote, "Where the focus goes, your power flows." Wherever your focus goes, my focus is on the positive aspects, so my power goes in that direction. It doesn't mean that I'm perfect, it just means that I'm "becoming."

Can you think of a scenario where you've worked with someone that you taught them Accurate Thinking, and then they experienced a transformation in their life?

Johnnie Lloyd: I did some classes for teenagers about money. What they learned is how to connect time and money, because they had the two separated. Now, they're more accurately thinking and bridging the connection. They're being more time-conscious, which is going to help in their futures. A couple people in the class said it had already impacted their TV watching and what they were doing on their phones. They have realized there's a fight for our time and money, and that we have to control it.

I won't say who, but I worked with a person who had a more powerful impact. They were a major leader in the community. I listened to them and ask them challenging questions. Internally, they had the answer already, but they just needed to get to it. So, their personal life became better. Even though they were an extreme public success, their personal life was pretty jacked up. Once they became more self-aware, they moved from being stuck in some areas and growing their personal life. Then their actions were different, and they ended up with a greater peace of mind. It has really impacted them relationally and financially.

Working with people like you do, I'm sure that becomes a really rewarding part of your impact, and career, to see that these principles are working, but also that you got to play a part in that, right?

Johnnie Lloyd: Right, absolutely. The funny thing is these principles had to work in my life first. Now I've become my own advertisement. I start telling my story, or part of my story. Then I get such a sense of peace and resolve when I know that I have impacted someone else's life.

When you saw that, I'm sure that's what inspired you to become a Napoleon Hill Certified Leader. What do you think some tips or words of encouragement would be if someone else is considering becoming a Certified Leader as well? What would you say to encourage them?

Johnnie Lloyd: I would say go do it, if they're looking for something and they don't know really what it is, especially if they're gifted in a lot of areas but they want to know what they should take their total focus on. Napoleon Hill's principles teach you to be selfless, not selfish. It's about giving back to the community. It's about giving to people. It's about making your life better and helping others make their lives better.

If somebody's looking for the purpose in their life and looking for something beyond just typical success, or what people may call success, I would tell them to go after it, even if it's only for themselves. Because when I started, my search was really personal. I became a certified instructor only once I realized the impact it had on me.

What would you say the five-step implementation or action plan would be for the Principle of Accurate Thinking?

Johnnie Lloyd: One, tell the person to think about how they think. Two, choose what they want to achieve then go in and make a plan on how to achieve it, as they move forward. Remember that accurate thinkers are critical thinkers. When they look at books and radio, TV, all this media, just think about it. Then be self-aware. Three, use self-reflection—look at the who, the what, the when, the where, and the how in their lives—and connect it to that. Four, take control of their own life. The mind is a mainframe computer of their life, and if they only put garbage in, they're only going to get garbage out. Make no excuses. Five, go back to Principle #2 from Napoleon Hill, and build a Mastermind Alliance that will help you grow.

Every person deserves success, and success should not be built on other people's opinions. It's based on what success is for us, so take control of your own mind and release your own personal greatness.

Are you a female executive or leader who desires to take your life and or organization to the next level? Do you want greater, but there is a gap to getting there? Are you so good at everything but want to know your purpose, your place of greatness? We help guide you into your next level success - from the inside out.

About Johnnie Lloyd

Johnnie is the Chief Visionary Officer and President of Johnnie Lloyd and Associates and successful serial entrepreneur. She is a servant leader who exudes great love and passion for people. Her definite major purpose is to impact lives, especially women in such a way that higher levels of greatest is unleashed.

She is a highly experienced visionary that specializes in Transformational Development by utilizing proven success principles. She has extensive experience as a Fiscal Executive with over 35 years of expertise. She engages her audiences as a Speaker who has went from homelessness to a builder of wealth. She is a master Facilitator, Coach, Trainer, and Consultant who continues to demonstrate innate ability to facilitate, build, and lead diverse teams to new levels of success in a variety of interactive and engaging ways. Johnnie is a global powerhouse who is a captivating professional with impeccable character and integrity. She is known as a financial Guru "Pusher" who can take financial and other leadership concepts then congruently connect with everyone regardless of their financial background stress, or fears regarding finances. Currently she volunteers training classes and some personalized financial review/coaching for a nonprofit organization that specializes in serving our Veterans in Virginia, providing classes such as Budgeting: Time and Money; Building Self-Confidence; and Self-Discipline.

After retiring to Purpose in 2017 her focus is walking out her definite major purpose. She works from the premise that people are the key to great organizations culture, performance, process, products, and or service. She enjoys creating limitless opportunities for others, based on maximizing their potential through proven principles that are unleashed from right where they are, with what they have. Her motto is "You are fire when you are focused"™ and "Transforming your mind transforms your world and money."

Learn More: www.JohnnieLloyd.com

Principle #11: Controlled Attention – Interview with Grant Campbell

---

Concentration, itself is nothing but a matter of control of the attention. Learn to fix your attention on a given subject, at will, for whatever length of time you choose, and you will have learned the secret passageway to power and plenty! This is CONCENTRATION.
~ Napoleon Hill

Why is the Principle of Controlled Attention relevant for today?

Grant Campbell: I think everyone would agree that the distractions that exist today make Controlled Attention—or learning how to have laser-like focus, in regard to the attainment of what your goals are, or what your purpose is—as important today as it ever was.

It's an important topic because there are people out here that are trying to get the most out of themselves. It becomes obvious that in order to achieve, we need to be able to reduce the distractions. Everyone is looking to be more effective and more efficient at what we do. Without Controlling your Attention and what you allow your senses to latch onto, your effectiveness in the workplace—and your personal effectiveness, too—is reduced greatly.

That's a matter of really being aware, correct?

Grant Campbell: Yes. Awareness is important but keeping your Purpose in mind is vitally important because there are some things that aren't deserving of your immediate attention. It doesn't mean that those aren't also important things, but those aren't things that you necessarily need to focus on at this moment in order to accomplish what it is that you set out to accomplish.

You need to know where that compass is pointing because you can feel like you're putting focused Attention and Controlled Attention on this matter at hand, but the bigger question actually is "will that lead you to the next step of where you need to be?"

What misconceptions are out there surrounding the Principle of Controlled Attention?

Grant Campbell: There is a difference between hearing something and absorbing it; being exposed to something and completely understanding what it is that's being presented.

A lot of times we hear things, and we think that we are paying attention, but we're really not concentrating on what either the speaker is saying or what the meaning is that's being conveyed, and that can be through the writing of something, or the listening of something. We all have situations and times where people have spoken to us, and we heard them, but then later we couldn't repeat or couldn't tell you what they said.

We've had situations where we've read things, and understood what we read, but we didn't retain it. In other words, we weren't really paying Attention. Your eyes were reading the words, or your ears were hearing the words, but you were not assimilating the information. In both hypnosis and in psychology, it's called a scotoma. You can literally see something, but it's not registering.

You made such a huge point about two things. Number one, having that Definiteness of Purpose in mind and knowing where you're heading, so that your attention is pointing the right way. And then not just hearing things, or seeing things, or noticing things, but aligning that with that purpose, so that people can realize, "Yeah, this is the path I need to take because this will get me closer to my goal," or "This aligns with my Purpose, so this is where I need to have my attention."

Grant Campbell: Absolutely. A lot of the spiritual practices of the East involve themselves greatly in developing concentration and teaching the difference between just hearing (being present when something is presented) and absorbing (being able to understand the essence of the material itself that's being presented). There is a difference between contemplation and concentration which is a point to study as well. But I believe Controlled Attention is a concept that brings to life all the other Principles of the system that Napoleon Hill created.

How much do you think technology impacts that?

Grant Campbell: I can't blame technology. I can say that, from my experience and observations, technology has created a situation where people have developed habits that allow technology to become a hindrance to paying Attention. It's not technology itself, because you don't have to choose to use technology in a way that is distracting you. You can have habits that are quite to the contrary and set limits for yourself.

But what happens with most people, and this greatly affects children when parents are unaware—as many parents are—is the visual stimulation that kids get from the high tech, the high definition, and the changing environment that we're producing with the greater graphics, and all of that, alters their interest and Attention, so, when you ask them to study or "pay attention" in a traditional sense to give their focus to a teacher who is trying for 15 minutes to explain a point, they're not accustomed to doing that. Looking at a blackboard is different than watching a monitor with hi-def graphics, don't you think?

Adults, likewise, have adopted habits and standards based upon this technology. 30 years ago, there was no option to get an immediate response from someone that you were trying to connect to. You couldn't call them on the cell phone, or do things like texting, so we've adopted different standards and habits as a result of technology. That's a decision that everyone has to make for themselves.

I've seen people get into really harsh arguments with one another because they didn't return phone calls. The person called them five or six times, and certainly felt offended that their phone calls weren't returned. But when you look at the fact that they called them five or six times in the span of 15 minutes on a cell phone, and the expectation was to be able to reach them no matter where they are, that comes down to our expectations and how we choose to use technology. Not how technology is, per se.

What positive changes did you experience in your life after applying the Principle of Controlled Attention to your personal and business life?

Grant Campbell: I believe this is something the most successful people constantly work on and are aware of. Certainly, for myself, as I got older and matured, I understood the importance of being able to maximize my performance and my learning in various areas, so understanding Controlled Attention just enhanced the things that I was able to do and to attain. It's something that facilitates the learning process.

Also, in athletics, it means that you're not wasting your time or that you're not wasting energy on things that are not leading to the desired outcome.

Can you share an example of how you have helped a client overcome these obstacles and succeed in using Controlled Attention in their personal or business life?

Grant Campbell: As a teacher, I get people that are brought to me that have been diagnosed with ADD, ADHD, and a variety of other syndromes that have interfered with their performance in school. By teaching them about how to focus their energy, and how to direct their energy on the subject at hand, and eliminating the distracting elements—which could, at times, be sounds, physical stimulation, verbal situations, or verbal distractions— then they can perform completely differently. When you teach someone consciously how to eliminate those things, not focus their mind on them, not allow them to disrupt their Attention, they can perform better. I've done that for many, many people over a lot of years.

I had a student that is a professional entertainer. Prior to learning the Principle, his energy was all over the place, but then he noticed that, as he got more focused in his sessions with me and as he started to learn, he was able to apply that same focus to his music. Seeing that for himself was motivating so he easily increased his intensity in practice. So, in the end, he was able to really make progress in a way that he hadn't done before. He attributed his study with me to that success.

I think what Napoleon Hill is saying in some of the Principles is that dabbling is quite different than mastery. People often confuse the two. They don't really understand that someone who is truly a master of something is someone who knows how to apply their energy to a given task.

That's why, in the East, they say that mastery of one thing can lead to mastery of many things, because the way that you approach studying something in order to attain a high level of skill teaches you a lot about how to get the most out of yourself. And in doing so, you're able to apply that Principle to other things, and it helps you get the most out of yourself as you apply it to that thing as well. I hope that makes sense.

Bruce Lee said, "I fear not the man who has practiced 10,000 kicks once, but I fear the man who has practiced one kick 10,000 times." Martial Arts is a wonderful way of increasing your ability to do that.

What do you think an implementation action plan is for the Principle of Controlled Attention?

Grant Campbell: In order to practice and develop Controlling your Attention, I think a few things would be helpful. One would be to understand that this something that needs to be applied gradually. Increase the intensity and the strength of your focus in small ways, gradually. Make a note, or a list of things that you find yourself distracted by, because awareness can sometimes be curative. If you are aware that those are your triggers and those are things that you allow to distract your Attention, you can sometimes avoid those very things because you're now aware of them. You can classify them and put them in their proper place.

The practices of meditation and exercise are all proven to help to develop your Attention if you do them and other activities that encourage mindfulness. That's a very big area and topic that can be developed, and will definitely help in Controlling your Attention, your ability to focus.

About Grant Campbell

Grant Campbell is an internationally renowned teacher, coach, a multiple business owner and author.

He's taught and coached thousands to achieve outstanding results in various areas of life. With a genuine interest in the growth and development of his clients that few in the industry possess, Grant truly lives and works with passion.

Learn more at www.grantcampbell.net

Principle #12: Teamwork– Interview with Lefford Fate

There is no record of any great contribution to civilization without the cooperation of others
~Napoleon Hill

Lefford, can you discuss why the Principle of Teamwork is relevant for today?

Lefford Fate: The bottom line is that Teamwork makes the dream work. In my favorite book, there's a passage that says, "The one may be overpowered, two can defend themselves, and a cord of three strands is not easily broken." Some of you may figure out where I got that from. (It's Ecclesiastes 4:12.) One of the things I learned by being in the military is that I cannot do it alone. Your team is what's going to help you win in anything. I've been deployed on number of occasions out there in the battlefield and have been deployed in remote locations. The people around me, my team, is what helped me survive when times got hard. With the right team, you can do anything that you want to do. The wrong team can make your life miserable. Teamwork is extremely important in everything that we do.

We can think of Teamwork in business, too, because there are business teams that you work in to accomplish a project. What would you say to someone in selecting "the right team"?

Lefford Fate: Well, I think it's the same thing. It could be family. It could be friends. It can be many things. When you talk about Teamwork, somebody that you're working with to get a job done, you're coming together with a definite goal toward what you're working for. That's how I look at it. It doesn't have to be just this or that. It can be anything where two or more people are getting together to accomplish any mission.

A misconception on the whole process is that many people today think that, they could do it all by themselves. Or they think that if you're on a team, you can hide and somebody else can do the stuff that you don't want to do. For me, Teamwork means that every person who is on that team learns to do their job well. The best Teamwork anthem is the Pledge of Allegiance. It starts with "I" and ends with "all." It takes all of us to make a country, each individual person. Each person has to be able to and be willing to do their job, to carry their own load, but realize that they got people on their team that can help them when they need it.

Do you feel the misconception is, "I've got my team"... but they either consciously or subconsciously are thinking, "I'm going to do the minimal amount of work possible because all these other people are the work"?

Lefford Fate: When I was in grad school, most of the projects that I was on had some people that just did the bare minimum. Some people weren't going to do anything. Some people wanted to run the whole show. Yes, I see that a great deal. Sometimes I see people who want to do things, but they're not confident in themselves, so they don't do what they desire to do. Some people just don't trust others, and they want to run the whole show. I've seen all those different outcomes. What I recognized was that's just the normal process of the Teamwork process. Take group dynamics. You still, as an individual, need to do your part. Everybody needs to do their part.

Now one of the things that I think is—and I'm not going to call it a misconception; I'm going to call it a mistake—I think a lot of people, when they're putting their team together, put together people that are just like them—who sees things like them, and thinks like them. I think that's a huge mistake. You must have the same end goal. If everybody thinks the same way, that can get you into "group think," and somebody is not going to see the roadblocks or those blind spots. You need to have somebody who can see a little bit differently, even though you're working for the same goal.

That's a really, good point. You need to know a little bit about yourself when you're assembling your team, so you can see where some gaps are. Do you feel that someone needs to find someone on their personal team, or their advisory team, who would complement their weakness with the person's strength?

Lefford Fate: It may sound aggressive, but I think that's 100% what you want to do. You need to pick your team based on your desired outcome. You decide what you want, and then make a decision on who joins that team. For example, I'm a basketball player and I like winning. Now I'm 6'2". If I really want to win the game, I'll need to get a seven-footer. I'll need maybe someone who is 5'8" to 6'2" that can run the ball and shoot and all that, but I'm not just going to go grab five Shaquille O'Neals. I need somebody else to fill different roles. Where I'm weak, somebody else is strong—that's how you build your team.

One of the things that people make a mistake on is that they don't want to hurt people's feelings. They'll have somebody on their team that's not the right fit. Now, you can't choose your family. That's not the team that you want to go, "Yeah, I'm going to trade you for a newer model," but for business and for friends and all that stuff, if you're putting together something, you need the right people on your team. You need to be courageous enough to figure out who that is, and to ask people what they bring to the table.

Going a little level deeper, this Principle is called Teamwork, and a lot of people focus on the root word, the word "team." They let the "work" part in, but not too much. So, maybe, it needs to be Teamwork with "work" in all capitals—like TeamWORK or TEAMWORK!

Lefford Fate: Exactly. I'm 100% there because, again, think about it: We want a bunch of people on our team because we want to party and have fun, but the WORK part is what gets things done. Who can do this thing well? Who is the person that's most qualified to get it done? Those are the people that you put on your team—the people that will do the work. You got some people that are really, really smart, but they don't have the technical competence to do something. You might have to get that person. That's the "idea" person, but you may also have to have those people that actually go out there and put the rubber to the road. I think that's just huge.

Consider building a personal team and you have a couple people that you rely on for mentorship and—health, finances— sometimes the work is just being there and being accountable, being supportive, showing up for a coffee meeting, it's just the work of being engaged.

Lefford Fate: Right, because—think about it—Teamwork in a family is not necessarily doing the actual physical labor stuff. My wife, the kids, and I all have things that we are gifted at and the things that we can do, but we all got to put in the work to get stuff done. Nobody should feel they're just hangers-on, or somebody just feels they're doing all the work. That causes problems and friction in the in that Teamwork or family unit.

Everybody has to be able to do their part, and that part needs to be defined. Many times, we get ourselves in trouble when we have expectations that we've not articulated. For example, "I think you should be doing this, but I think I should be doing something else" are the things that get families and other teams in a lot of trouble.

As a Napoleon Hill Certified Coach and Leader, you work with clients. Can you think of an example of someone you've worked with that has maybe not seen the clear picture of Teamwork, and then once you've helped coach them and guide them through it, they've seen some breakthroughs?

Lefford Fate: Yes. Something came about in 2014, when I went to work for the Department of Corrections. The first thing that came on my desk was a discrimination complaint on one facility, where there were about 15 nurses, social workers, doctors, and admin people that were just not playing well together. It was a hostile work environment, and they weren't working well together. Discord in a prison setting can be dangerous. It can cost people their lives. We were at the point where we were going to fire a bunch of people. We were going to have to bring in other consultants to make it happen.

What we did was we started Teamwork training: how to be a team member. One of the things that I found that may be very surprising to you is that the average person, unless they played some type of sport, was not taught how to be a good teammate. We started from the beginning and had discussions on: What does Teamwork look like? What's your responsibility to the team? Who are you responsible to? Who are you responsible for? Because there's a difference. You're responsible to do something to give your best, to work hard to be a part, but you're also responsible for yourself. There are different things.

We turned around a group of people who we were going to disband. People went from "those who were going to lose their job" to "being one of the most highly-functioning teams in South Carolina Department of Corrections."

I had 640 people on staff, and this was the worst of the worst. They ended up becoming the best of the best because they actually learned. They decided—and that's the beautiful part about it, because they knew the deal: they could accept the training, or they could just whitewash it—but these people decided that they were going to be on the team. They were going to be good teammates. They were going to work to get through this thing. To me, that was amazing, because it's really good to share, but it's really great when the people that you share with take that on as their mission and go out there and put it in and become a winning team.

Teamwork is so important in working to get strengths and weaknesses aligned. What do you think an implementation action plan is for this Principle?

Lefford Fate: I have a program out there called (PH) REAL. I'm going to use (PH) REAL to talk about Teamwork. I'll just call it Teamwork (PH) REAL. The first thing is (PH) is Philosophy. What is your Philosophy about your team? You must decide what the team means to you. Is it the goal or the role? Is the goal of the team more important in your particular role, or is your role more important than a goal? You must make that decision, so determine your Philosophy.

R is for Relationship. That is the next part. Develop your Relationship because relationships matter. You have to get to know the people that you're working with on your team, what their strengths are, what their weaknesses are, what their likes and what they don't like. If you can figure out and develop great relationships, then your team is going to be better.

The E part of that is you have to Equip yourself. Everybody on the team must be equipped to do their particular job the best. When they do that job the best, individually, then they can support the rest of the team. You have to Equip yourself, and then you have to Equip your teammates, not only in the individual test, but as the team.

A is for Attitude. You need the right positive attitude. We talked about Positive Mental Attitude. Believe in the team. Believe that they can. And think. You could think positively, and you could think negatively. If you think positive, with a Positive Mental Attitude, you'll get things done. If you think negative, you won't get things done. Ask yourself, "What am I going to do to have the best attitude to go out there to win?"

The last part is L is for Lead. You need to Lead the team well. Every member of that team must Lead. The first person that you're responsible to Lead is yourself. How can you lead yourself first, to be there on time, to getting it done, to making everything work? Then you lead the people on your team, because you know everybody doesn't have the same level of leadership. But everyone has leadership. Influence is leadership. Leadership is the influence. You have to you have to Lead well.

Decide what you want in the beginning. It's almost like this. You have to decide you want to go to New York, before you just jump in the car start driving. What is that goal that you're working toward? Make that decision and know that everybody can't be on your team. You have to make a decision of who the right people are for your team. If you take the time to decide to put the right people on your team, then that team will be successful.

If you get the wrong apple, the bad apple on that team, you need to have the courage to remove that person from that team. They may be a good person, they may be a good person in the sight of God, but they may not be the right person for your team. You have to make that decision. That's what I feel is what gets you towards having great Teamwork and a team that works.

You have met your Fate; let's walk into your destiny.

About Lefford Fate

Professionally I've led, mentored, and served thousands of military members and their families during my 30 years in the United States Air Force.

Since retiring from the military, I have been the program director for the geriatric outpatient mental health program, deputy Director for Health Services, SC Department of Corrections,

and now the Director Support Services, City of Sumter.

I am a husband, father, and grandfather, so I know it is not always easy to juggle our list of daily responsibilities. This makes it even more important to have a structured, practical plan in place to avoid becoming overwhelmed. I hold a Master's Degree in Human Relations and a Bachelor's Degree in Social Psychology. Modeling the core values of Integrity first, Service before self and Excellence in all I do.

I believe there is a "why" for everyone; that each of us was created with the potential to achieve greatness, to make a difference

in the world, to add value to others, and as a result, experience a full and rewarding life. For over 30 years, my purpose was to defend our nation, and now that purpose is helping people discover their life's purpose and grow to their full potential.

Learn More: http://www.leffordfate.com

Principle #13: Learning from Adversity and Defeat – Interview with Rae Brown

---

Don't fear defeat, it may reveal to you powers you didn't know you possessed.
~Napoleon Hill

Rae, why is the Principle of Learning from Adversity and Defeat relevant for today?

Rae Brown: The Principle, or the law, that we call Learning from Adversity and Defeat, is pretty much the entire concept of "If you don't win now, keep going." It's the law that covers the whole idea of not letting something that goes wrong in your plans stop you from getting to your goal.

Things happen in life. Life is always in session. If the session isn't a good session, don't let that session stop the whole realm of things for your life. Don't let it be the one thing that keeps you from your destiny. Things happen in life, bottom line. When Defeat comes in, you have to realize that it is not there to kill you. This may be something that allows you to see something a lot differently. It may even check your heart, it may check your character, or it may check something else in you. Defeat isn't really about losing. Adversity isn't really about losing. It's about what it's bringing to you. It's a gift; a gift given back to you. However, we always misconstrue it because we think it's there to hurt us.

Sometimes, we don't realize how great we are or what we possess, until we have to deal with Defeat or Adversity, or until we need to be resilient. If you play acoustic guitar, with steel strings, the "Adversity" is that your fingers pressing down on steel strings hurts, when you first start learning how to play. After a period of time, callouses build up and you get thicker skin on your fingertips. It, literally, is a thicker skin, and then it doesn't hurt to play. To take it a step further, the thicker skin also allows you to produce the sounds and vibrations that reverberate when you play. It connects with the people who you're playing the music for. It allows them to ascend. So, it contributes to the universal component of making music. We can apply that to life—to have thicker skin about most things!

Where do you feel that perseverance ties in to learning from Adversity and Defeat?

Rae Brown: I like the fancy word "perseverance." However, if you grew up in my town, it was called "grit." You must realize that no one is coming to rescue you. You need to rely on yourself to get things done, if you are the only one who can do it. That's that Definiteness of Purpose that we need to understand. Once we have that, no one else can do that work for you. They can cheer you on, they can want it for you, they can pray for you, and they can invest in you. They can do all that. However, that point is your thumbprint in life. If you're not persevering, if you're not showing your gumption, if you're not being resilient, if you're not Mario in the game "Super Mario," you won't overcome Adversity and Defeat. You just keep going on, and you keep going on until you are successful.

Perseverance is one of the most important skills of today because everything else is instant. The coffee is instant, the food is instant, and the love is instant. We misinterpret the process of getting things done, and part of that process is dealing with Adversity and Defeat. Napoleon Hill says nobody wins all the time, but I'm a firm believer that you don't have to lose all the time, either.

How do you train yourself to be present and to observe, "That was Adversity, that was Defeat, and I need to learn from it?"

Rae Brown: The one thing that I pride myself on is that I'm an implementation specialist.

The first thing that must happen is you must stop the velocity, the noise, and the whispers, and just get to a point where your velocity is slowed down enough to realize what just happened. You really have to stop and look and recognize what this is really echoing to you. Ask yourself, "What is this thing, or this lack of opportunity, or this block, or this stumbling saying to me?"

If you don't have a good voice in your head, or if you don't have other things in place, it can oftentimes be very deceiving. It can sound almost like the ping that you send out from a submarine, that bounces back to let you know that something is amiss. When it bounces back to you, you get to interpret what it is. Once you recognize it, you have to ask, "Is this a part of me? Is this my doing? Is it something out of my control? Is it something that I can actually bounce back from, or should I side-step it?" It really depends on what kind of strategist you are, and how invested you are in the things that you do. At that point, get to really define what it is. If it's a stumbling block, then you need to re-up—what I call re-up—which is to look at your Definiteness of Purpose and then take a sledgehammer and turn the stumbling block into stepping-stones. Or you could do something different, depending on what it means to you.

What misconceptions are out there surrounding the Principle of Learning from Adversity and Defeat?

Rae Brown: We personalize it. We take it personally. We feel like there's some big brother, or some bad guy, or some guy with a red suit on holding a pitchfork that's after us, and it's not going to allow us to get where we need to go on our journey. However, the focal lens must be corrected, because, if we really understand life—and most of us don't, because we're living it—it's all through retrospect. We realize, "It wasn't really something that would kill me. It really wasn't something to destroy me. It really was more about what I needed, at that time." I call this the MRI of life—Learning from Adversity and Defeat. It gives us the MRI of life to who we are, and it shows us, extensively, who we are and what we're made of. It gives us the power or the gumption to get back up again. And this process can be very time-consuming. We must realize what it is saying to us and then be able to be able to verbalize it in our own language.

What positive changes did you experience in your life after applying this Principle to your personal and business life?

Rae Brown: Without giving you my whole story, one of the things that I always go back to in my life is that I was raised in an adoption home and I was the only one that wasn't adopted. Everybody else got adopted, and they had their other families. However, my original family kept coming to get me, every weekend. What happened was, in my 20s, I started trying to put all this together, because all the messages being sent to me said, I wasn't worth it. My self-worth was low, my self-esteem was low, and I didn't have direction. I started internalizing this and I started going down a dark road. I come from a Christian background. One of the Scriptures talks about the adoption into the Lord, in the New Testament. And I realized what actually happened to me was the fact that the Lord was trying to show me, naturally, what's happening to me, spiritually.

This allowed me to switch the pendulum and say nothing or no one gets to dictate or gets to write my chapters or my story, but me. I then decided to start looking at things differently, and it was always easy because it was the voices of all those fears—that fear of success, the fear of failing—talking back to me, like goblins.

Then I realized they were lying to me, so I started doing the work of trying to find out, "How is this really helping me?"

Doing this has helped me in business, as an entrepreneur. I'm a funeral director, so people have to die for me to do business. Now, I don't know if you've ever waited for somebody to die, but that's not really a common thing that people wait for. Then, when people did die, and they didn't come to me, even though I know the family, it didn't serve me. However, what I learned is that I get to serve people that believe in who I am, as opposed to taking it personally. So, I think that is what has echoed back to me, which has allowed me to move forward with this law of not being taken over by Defeat and Adversity.

Can you share an example of how you have helped a client overcome these obstacles and succeed in using Learning from Adversity and Defeat in their personal or business life?

Rae Brown: Yes. I pastored for twelve years, and I considered myself a world-changer pastor. What that meant was, whoever I came into contact with, I assisted. However, I dealt a lot with individuals that were dealing with substance abuse, and there's this whole concept that it's a disease. However, part of the process of recovery is going back and having encounters with drugs and alcohol—with the addictive thing—again. A lot of times, when people fall prey to that, after they've had some time of success, it really becomes devastating because they can't understand it. So, they begin to beat themselves up and they go through this whole process again.

I once had a husband and wife team that had gotten to a point where they were getting it together. However, they were sabotaging other areas of their life. I began to talk to them and show them that, "Hey, you know what? Just because you can't get a job, or just because you didn't pass this test, or just because your boss gave you a bad review, doesn't mean this is an opportunity to fall prey again. Look at what you've accomplished. You've come this far. Look at your stepping-stones and begin to count your blessings."

The Scriptures didn't say to count your mistakes; it says to count your blessings. Oftentimes, this allows the heart to become grateful. It fills the space of the bad attitude with the positive, and it allows you to stay positive.

What inspired you to become a Napoleon Hill Certified Leader?

Rae Brown: One of the things that helped me (and my other colleagues) become a Certified Leader is that I met Napoleon Hill's grandson in New York, by accident. I ran into him at a book show at the Javits Center. I had heard of Hill's book, *Think and Grow Rich*, but I hadn't read it. I was coming up the escalators and I said to myself, "What would be a company—or who—should I look for?" That is kind of that *Think and Grow Rich* thing and is exactly what I said. As soon as I got off the escalator, who did I walk into but Napoleon Hill's Grandson.

He let me know who he was and began to speak to me about the philosophy. What I realized, what really kept pushing me—and this is over a five-year period of time, this wasn't instant because I just wasn't in the right frame of mind—is that it allowed me to begin to read and realize what Napoleon Hill's Think and Grow Rich philosophy was, and it gave me a plank to cross over. It allowed me that spiritual plank where I needed to say, "Hey, here are some laws. Here is something that is written." Also, what inspired me was the first one. It wasn't a copy of a copy of a copy. It wasn't someone's interpretation of his stuff. It was the plank, it was from him, it was the sausage. And I truly believe that my life has always been one of a forerunner, and one of the people that goes first.

What do you think an implementation action plan is for the Principle of Learning from Adversity and Defeat?

Rae Brown: The one thing I like to say, and I said it a little earlier, is there is an echo of what's being done or what is done. From that, I believe the first step is to stop and slow your velocity down. This is really all about you—the person. Once you stop and you get your velocity, you start understanding what happened. You must begin to look at it and recognize it, and determine if this was something to help you, or empower you. If it is, recognize that component of it, that seed that Napoleon Hill talks about. You got to get the seed. He didn't say it was a tree. He didn't say it was a plant. It's a seed.

It may be minuscule, but it can take you to the first step of what I call "re-up." That means go back to your Definite Purpose. What are you here for? What's your destiny? What's your mandate?

From there, you have to strategize again, and that strategy may take some time, because you might have to deal with *you*. You may have to seek wisdom and hear voices from other people who can support you and what you're doing.

The last thing, as difficult as it is, is be a winner. Pain, setbacks, defeats, and losses come. They're all misfortunes and we all suffer them. But the one thing we can't do is lose. Remember, count your blessings.

About Rae Brown

Rae Brown is a multi-talented professional with a multi-faceted background as a speaker, talk show host, spiritual leader and teacher, counselor, coach and educator.

Known for being a "leader's leader," Rae has cultivated her life-long mantra "Live MORE...fear less" into a movement of successful living and living on purpose.

Equipped with decades of experience, particularly as a counselor, coach and spiritual leader, and with her expertise in engaging audiences, Rae has impacted the lives of many individuals – from children to adults – exposing them to the tools needed to begin living their lives for "the MORE!" As a "Life Speaker," Rae delivers life-changing keynotes, presentations, and seminars with clarity and candor that her audiences never forget. Rae leads with her passion for helping people identify and live out their best, most purposed selves.

In 2014, Rae launched her television talk show, Live More with Rae. Anchored by her 20 years of counseling experience and her Live More Inventory which also emanates from her "Live MORE...fear less" philosophy, the show addresses life's issues through a blend of compelling interviews, inspiring human-interest stories, and empowering insights into life-transforming events.

As the show's creator, executive producer and host, Rae ministers to her guests and her viewers by exploring purposeful living as it relates to some of life's core components – spirituality, well-being, personal development, relationships, career, and finances. Currently broadcast on multiple cable networks in New Jersey and New York, Live More with Rae is a platform for others to see their truest selves through the art of conversation and in the mirror of experience.

Learn More: http://www.livemorewithrae.com

Principle #14: Creative Vision – Interview with Alejandro Manuel Miranda Torres

> *The Imagination is the workshop of the soul wherein are shaped all plans for individual achievement.*
> *~Napoleon Hill*

Alejandro, why is the Principle of Creative Vision relevant for today?

Alejandro: New technologies of modern times and all scientific inventions are the result of Creative Vision. Creative Vision is responsible for the civilization of today as we know it. Creative Vision inspires men and women to experiment with new ideas in every field or endeavor. It is always looking for better ways of doing man's labor and supplying human needs. Creative Vision makes human progress possible. It creates benefits for all humankind, improving all conditions on planet Earth.

Wherever men and women with Creative Vision are found, there also will be found progress, prosperity, and high standards of living.

What specifically would Creative Vision look like if you were telling someone, one on one, "Hey, we need to help you create Creative Vision in your life"? What would you be explaining to them?

Alejandro: Creative Vision is not only imagining things. Creative Vision must be accompanied by a Definite Major Purpose. More than just Creative Vision by itself, the application of other Principles is needed. That's why Napoleon Hill's success philosophy is so amazing—it invites you to combine Definite Major Purpose, a Mastermind Alliance, Going the Extra Mile, Personal Initiative, Enthusiasm, and Applied Faith.

What are some common misconceptions people have regarding the Principle of Creative Vision?

Alejandro: A great misconception is that we cannot create it just by dreaming or imagining or thinking. We need action. We need to apply action. In the achievement of every goal or Purpose, we need to have determination, persistence, and organized planning. We must work our plan and plan our work, and that means taking action.

I commonly find that people are sometimes not eager to live intentionally. That's the worst achievement—not having an intention in life and living with these Principles. I believe this philosophy is like cooking a cake. You have to add all the ingredients in order to get your Definite Major Purpose.

What positive changes did you experience in your life after applying this Principle to your personal and business life?

Alejandro: When I began reading *Think and Grow Rich* and all the back works of Napoleon Hill, I discovered there are two types of imagination: synthetic and creative. Synthetic imagination is the result of combining preexisting concepts, facts, plans, or ideas and Creative Vision or creative imagination is having direct communication with infinite intelligence. This is the faculty through which conscious inspirations are received. What I mean by this is that I have learned to never neglect the hunch or intuition in my life. I understand now that *will* comes in response to one's Definite Major Purpose, based in the application of the definite Principles we just spoke about. And nothing happens just by chance or luck.

All of my professional life, I have been in the world of logistics, supply chain management, the transportation of goods internationally, port operations, and all that. Some years ago, we opened a new office for our company in the Pacific Ocean in Mexico, in a small port named Manzanillo, which happens to be the biggest port in Mexico. I understood that I needed to be creative in order to have a competitive advantage, and present and offer solutions to my clients. So, we combined two existing ideas, which nobody else was using together. Our creativity made those plans and protocols, and we were able to offer new ideas and new solutions to our client. For instance, it normally took seven days to release a container at the port. After applying our creative concept, these new ideas allowed us to release our customer's containers in less than three days. That made us very competitive!

What inspired you to become a Napoleon Hill Certified Leader?

Alejandro: I consider myself a seeker. I have always been intrigued by success and the way to achieve it. When I first read *Think and Grow Rich*, I deeply connected with Hill's philosophy of personal achievement. I really felt inspired and excited about learning and living these Principles. I had been working very hard all my life, but there was something missing; something was not in its place. I decided to become certified because I wanted to be close to the Napoleon Hill Foundation. That meant a lot to me, because being close to the source and being there gave me a clearer vision of what I wanted to achieve.

What I learned is that I needed to add value to my life, to teach others to add value to theirs, and to inspire people to add value to humanity.

Can you think of a few initial steps for an action plan where people could start putting the Principle of Creative Vision into action in their lives?

Alejandro: Yes. I have a five-task plan that I have developed.

First, provide yourself with a Definite Major Purpose. It's important to have one because that is the first step for personal achievement.

Second, put your imagination to work on the building of a plan for the transformation of your desire into money. Write the plan, plan your work, and work your plan. Read it twice a day.

Three, write ten things daily that can help you achieve or improve your Definite Major Purpose.

Four, develop the habit of asking questions. For instance, I constantly ask myself things like, "What is my definition of success?" That gives me energy and it provides me with a wider perspective of life and success.

Five, adopt the habit of sitting silently for one hour a day. Have a pencil and paper close to you and write down whatever comes to mind. This last task is very important for implementing the Principle of Creative Vision.

About Alejandro Manuel Miranda Torres

- Logistics Professional
- Certified by Napoleon Hill Foundation
- Certified by John Maxwell Leadership Program
- Facilitator for Osho Active Meditations

Social Media Contact: @exitoAlejandro Miranda

Principle #15:
Maintenance of Sound Health –
Interview with Sandra Valencia

A Positive Mental Attitude aids in the development
of bodily resistance against disease
~Napoleon Hill

Sandra, why is the Principle of Maintenance of Sound Health so important today?

Sandra Valencia: Maintenance of Health is such an important Principle these days because so many diseases and illnesses are happening recently, and this is all due to not having a mind and body health consciousness. What I mean by "mind and body health consciousness" is that not all people have a Definite Purpose or goal in life, or something that they look forward to, except, perhaps, going to work and coming home to watch TV, and living this kind of sedentary life. I'm not saying everyone does the same thing, but a big percentage of the population do these very passive activities, which can create problems. They will have issues with fear, anxiety, and other worries because they don't have anything that excites them or makes them feel motivated. They don't have something to look forward to, such as a specific target or goals. That's basically why this Principle is so relevant in today's society.

You need to start by doing a small exercise, gradually, perhaps once or twice a week, and by choosing the right meals and keeping a Positive Mental Attitude. This is a good segue to talk a little bit about why the mind and body are sort of connected. It turns out, if you don't have a Positive Mental Attitude, and you don't have a Definite Purpose, then that's when you fall into having, perhaps, diseases.

When you think about Maintaining Sound Health, people tend to focus on just their body, correct? What misconceptions are out there surrounding this Principle?

Sandra Valencia: Basically, the misconception is that Sound Health is only having the absence of symptoms of illnesses. In reality, Sound Health is a positive state of well-being that encompasses the body, the mind, emotions, and all relationships— that's the whole; the mind and body connected. If I have resentment, I live by hating people. If I don't have a Positive Mental Attitude in all my relationships and about everything, then things will start falling apart. Consequently, this state of mind that is so negative will eventually transfer in a physical aspect and cause diseases or other health issues.

What positive changes did you experience in your life after applying the Principle of Maintenance of Sound Health to your personal and business life?

Sandra Valencia: I have an amazing example for this. A year ago, I went to the Napoleon Hill Worldwide Certified Leader Certification. At that time, I was overweight. After I went to the Napoleon Hill event, I decided that I was going to change my lifestyle. I understood that I needed to find my reason of why I wanted to lose weight. So, I asked myself, "Why do I want to lose weight? What motivates me?" I realized I want to feel healthy, I want to have more flexibility, and I want to look and feel thinner and better.

I then established short-term goals. The Napoleon Hill philosophy talks about Definite Purpose, but people can start by doing just a little, doing a short-term goal. My short-term goal was a three-month short-term goal. I established a very detailed plan for what I was going to eat, what I was going give up during that period, my exercise plan, and so on, and a target date. That kept me very motivated, and I lost 25 pounds.

I'm maintaining it because I did it gradually. Another Principle that is very key to being able to Maintain Sound Health is Self-Discipline. That really helped me a lot. Self-Discipline is basically willpower to be able to maintain this. And it's forever, it's not just a year thing, or three months. It's just being able to do it. So, I changed completely, everything—eating out, exercising, everything.

How does a gradual approach and Self-Discipline tie together?

Sandra Valencia: Actually, I have thought about this very much in a sense that I understand, because I also want to become fit. I've realized that you need to be patient with yourself. It took me two years or three years to gain the weight, so it's going to take me time to lose it and become fit.

It was due to stress that I gained all this weight. In a year, I've been able to lose 25 pounds, and I want to lose 10 more. I'm constantly telling myself, when I look at the mirror, "Wow, Sandra, you have done a great job." I motivate myself, but I need to understand when I'm exercising, that in order to be fit, I have to do a lot of exercise, and it's not going to happen overnight. If I gained that weight in two, three years, I'm not going to lose it in a year. It has to gradually change.

Nothing can be done overnight. If you do it gradually, then you will be more successful. You will be able to achieve your goal.

Can you share an example of how you have helped a client overcome these obstacles and succeed in using the Principle of Maintenance of Sound Health in their personal or business life?

Sandra Valencia: In terms of personal aspects, I have a very successful story about my mother, who, in the last couple years, has had three spinal cord surgeries. I have been applying this Principle amazingly in her life, in two aspects. In the aspect of eating, I have helped with changing her eating habits and making sure she loses weight, because she was a little overweight. Losing the weight helped reduce the inflammation and increase her self-esteem and different aspects of her health. The other aspect, the one that I've been working with, mostly, is her mind. I like to talk about the mind aspect because that is really tied to the physical, to the body. I've been working with her a lot with the practical formula from psychologist Emil Coue's methodology, which is based on affirmations and daily repetition. My mom and I both say all the time: "Every Day in Every Way, I'm getting better and better." This is helping with the mind and body connection.

I've also been looking at real stories in history of people who are disabled and have different kind of disabilities. My mother's legs are completely numb, and she walks with a walker. I said, "Listen, at this point, nobody is going to be able to help you because, in terms of doctors and what they can do, they did what they could do. So, now, you need to take responsibility for your health, and you need to work with mind and body connection and be able to tell yourself "Every Day in Every Way, I'm getting better and better." Mother, you're taking responsibility for your body and you're telling your body that your body is going to get better and better every day."

This psychologist used this through the years—and they even use it at prisons—and this was very successful. Doctors were really hesitant about this, but they were able to prove that this really works. This uses your conscious mind and calls in to the fact that, if you repeat yourself so many times through the day, eventually your body, and your subconscious mind will believe it. Even if it's true or not, the body will believe it.

What inspired you to become a Napoleon Hill Certified Leader and what words of encouragement would you give to others considering becoming one as well?

Sandra Valencia: What really inspired me to become a Napoleon Hill Certified Leader was, many years ago when I read *Think and Grow Rich*. When I read that book, it caught my attention—the focus on having a Definite Purpose in life, and the ability to understand that, if you can help other people, your life will be more fulfilled, and all the blessing that comes along with helping others. So, I started to get motivated in going to the program. The program has three steps, and when I took the first step of the program, it was to listen to all the Napoleon Hill live lectures, and it was presentations or audios. He said, in one of his speeches, "I want all of you to be able to carry my mission and spread it all over the world." So, I said, "I'm going to be one." I really got very excited about going into the program, and then decided to take the formal training.

I have a formal education, meaning I went to college and got a degree. College or academia is something that I encourage people to do as well. In addition to that It is important to work on your personal development. Napoleon Hill Principle of Success is about personal development, and we will not get anywhere if we don't develop those personal skills that will help us to interact with our families, to improve our relationships, to be able to be positive, and to interact with all our surroundings, with anybody that we encounter in our lives. Consequently, having better relationships.

What do you think an implementation action plan is for the Principle of Maintenance of Sound Health?

Sandra Valencia: The five steps that I'm going to mention will all help with the mind and body health consciousness.

The first step is to express gratitude and meditate for five to ten minutes, daily. There are many instructions on YouTube for how to do that, so anybody can find that information there. Using meditation and expressing gratitude on a daily basis will help with having a Positive Mental Attitude and bringing more blessings in our lives. Give thanks for what you have, not only for what you have, but also for what you want to have.

The second one is to use daily affirmations. Daily affirmations are very critical. I've been doing this for years. Daily affirmations help with one of the most negative things for a human being, which is fear. We're fearful about everything. I'm starting to improve my speaking skills, so, for example, a daily affirmation would be to say, "I'm a great speaker. I'm a great speaker!" I do this many times daily. How does the affirmations help to improve the mind and body health consciousness? This will help you with your fears and with all your worries. You're repeating yourself; you're telling yourself, "I'm good at this. I'm good at this." So, it will help you get yourself to the point that you're so confident that you will really be successful in being a great speaker.

The third one, which is very critical for Maintaining Sound Health of both mind and body is focusing on your Definite Purpose and setting goals. Set your goals and, as I mentioned earlier, do them or reach them gradually. I did a goal for three months, and I was able to achieve it. I was motivated. Set a goal that motivates you, excites you, and make a detailed plan, too, because if you have a detailed plan, a structured and organized plan, then that will help with anxiety.

The last four and five steps are to choose the right meals and have an exercise routine. You can also do intermittent fasting. Napoleon Hill talks about doing intermittent fasting twice a year for ten days but I think that's too much. He says he's not a doctor and I will say the same thing, but I've been doing—in addition to what I have established to Maintain Sound Health, mindful health—intermittent fasting. People can search this in YouTube; there are many videos and many doctors and experts are talking about this. So, that's basically what my action plan would be.

About Sandra Valencia

Sandra Valencia is a world-class Napoleon Hill Certified Leader. She is also Project Management Institute Project Management Professional Certified.

In her role as Senior Information Technology Program Manager for the U.S. government, she has written several project management processes and procedures for internal use. She very much enjoys her government work, but she is also very passionate about the power of the mind-body connection to maintain sound health, as well as the impact we can have in our bodies by maintaining health consciousness.

Sandra lives in Maryland and is the mother of two lovely children, Sebastian and Juliana Gonzalez-Valencia, and a daughter of the most amazing woman, Maria Ines Vargas de Valencia, who has used mind-body health consciousness to overcome her disability.

Sandra is looking forward to you reading her feature chapter "Maintain Sound Health." It is her hope that it will be helpful to you to learn how you can become more health conscious.

Social Media Contact: Facebook.com/sandra.valencia.7564

Principle #16:
Budgeting Time and Money
–Interview with Johnnie Lloyd

Tell me how you use your spare time and how you spend your money, and I will tell you where and what you will be 10 years from now.
~ Napoleon Hill

Johnnie, give us a little background on yourself, and what we are going to be in store for with this principle. What are you going to focus on with Budgeting Time and Money?

Johnnie Lloyd: I actually have over 40 years' worth of Budgeting or wealth management experience. When I say that, I'm including Time, Money, property, and all that kind of experience. I started off being homeless, and now I have degrees and certifications and all those wonderful things. However, what I want to encourage each one of us to do is realize it's all about taking our control back.

Most people don't look at Budgeting as something that gives them control of their life. They look at it as a negative. So, when we transfer that thought process, it causes us to build the tenacity, and the Enthusiasm to look at what we're doing, to get us what we really want. We use Time and Money that way. So, that's what this principle means to me.

This principle is probably one of the most powerful principles, because you need self-discipline and you need accuracy—and you need all of those the other principles in order to do this. But it can be fun. It doesn't have to be hard. It can be fun.

You said, "taking control back," one word that came to my mind was "confidence." Some people working through this Principle of Budgeting Time and Money will get it right the first time, but as they work at it and have that confidence to succeed, their levels will soar. They'll realize that their baby steps improved their lives, even if they don't make the perfect Budget and Money decisions initially.

Can you speak to how relevant this principle is for today as it relates to building confidence and even just in the economy that we're in today?

Johnnie Lloyd: Yes. One of the things that you mentioned was confidence, and confidence is built based on habit.

When you look at the economy today, a lot of people have always thought that the government or someone outside of themselves will take care of them in their old age. Now, we have to look at it very differently. The relevant point here is that we must see the person we're going to be in the future—our older self. If we don't see our older self by setting up, whether it be wealth management, whether it's setting aside money, whether it's buying property, or something to feed our older self, then what's going to happen is, we're losing our control.

We're depending on someone else to take care of us and the system has changed. What *was* set aside to take care of us is gone, so we really need to establish and take care of ourselves. Everything is moving where they're depending on your 401k. You need to put aside money, all of that. That's where Time and Money management, or Budgeting, comes in. Because wealth management is really about life management, and the confidence is about starting where you are.

Right now, you may not have any control. So, it's about starting where you are, and looking to see where you want to be, and then building upon that.

Yes, you're not going to be excellent at it the first time. But you will learn. Just like when a child tries walking and falls but gets up and tries again and again. That child is not told, "Okay, you can't walk anymore because you fell."

So, you need to allow yourself to go through that failing process. Failing allows us to grow and become better. As we become better, we see the results, and the results cause us to move forward. But you need to have a Definite Purpose and align everything to that Purpose.

Consider when you are an older person sitting on a porch swing, with your significant other, and/or family members, saying, "Wow, let me look back over my life. Look at all these things— I sure have had a fulfilled life. If you can picture and create that, it then becomes your Definite Purpose and it gives you a clear plan to work toward.

Johnnie Lloyd: Right. It *is* going to be some work. Yes, I have had a couple clients who have done and accomplished that. The way that they did it is by using vision boards—something you need to see with your eyes—and then going after it all with your actions.

Vision is the purpose, and you have to put a date on it, and you have to put an amount on it, and then you need to determine what you're willing to do in exchange for it.

A lot of people want it, so what I encourage people to do is to find out their "why." To do that, I tell them to ask that question five times to themselves and write out a deeper answer each time. By the time they get to the fifth time, they find out the real reason they want the wealth, or the real reason they want better health, or the real reason that they are willing to go through this process of building the habits (like telling yourself "no"). Self-discipline is what will help them to get to their end result, which may be swinging on a swing on your front porch that's paid for, or something where they can say, "I don't want to worry about that," or "I want my child to be able to go to school," or "I want to get out of debt."

Look at the reason—the purpose—and then look at the process of what you're willing to do to get there. That's it.

This is what I know about this principle. This principle, like all the other principles, is powerful because principles just work. Gravity is a principle. It's not based on me believing in gravity. Gravity just works, and you don't do anything. That's why Budgeting Time and Money is so important—because it's related to a principle.

We don't get any more time. We have the same 24 hours as Oprah or anybody else that's a billionaire or millionaire. It doesn't matter how much money you make; I still have my same 24 hours. The question is, what am I doing with it?

What are some misconceptions surrounding Budgeting Time and Money?

Johnnie Lloyd: One is that they believe it's easy, and if they do it one time, that will settle everything. Another misconception is that Budgeting Time and Money is for other people, or they don't have enough money to really do a budget, so they don't think that control mechanism is what they need. Or they feel like they're in too much debt, and they don't want to see it, so it's connected to fear. A lot of people don't do it because they're afraid of knowing where they're at.

But you can't be afraid. You have to face it. It's as simple as a GPS. If I want to get somewhere, I have to tell that system, that Global Positioning System, that works, where I am and where I want to go. So, if I don't know where I am, by Budgeting, I surely can't get there. So, the misconception—whether you're rich or poor, whether you work heavily in this principle—is that most people think, "I don't have enough time and I don't have enough money." But it's not just about having enough. It's about dealing with what you have.

That's a great point. Most of the time, when you hear people teaching and coaching specific things, such as principles that they've had success with, they probably have a little bit of a backstory and success, and can say, "Hey, I've failed in this, and here's how I succeeded."

From your perspective, what positive changes did you experience after applying Budgeting Time and Money to your life?

Johnnie Lloyd: I love the word, "backstory." A little bit about my backstory is that I had a degree. I was already educated, but having information is not enough. Being degreed is not enough, and having a good job is not enough to keep you away from this principle. So, I had all those things, and I became homeless. Now, there were some other dynamics, but I became homeless because I was running after things and not considering how much money we were actually making.

What happened is I learned this story the hard way.

Most of us have parents that showed us things, good and bad. My parents gave me great insight, and I knew a little bit about Napoleon Hill, so, that was my first introduction, in the 1970s. However, that didn't stop my process.

As I went through my process, I gathered more knowledge and I found out the Budgeting system. Because I'm an accountant, the Budgeting system I learned from the government is actually the same budgeting system I needed to implement in my house.

It caused me to do some things. What I found out, too, is it's not about how much money you make, it's about how much money you spend. If you make a million dollars, but you spend a million dollars and one, you're still over.

So, it's not about how much money you have. It's about what you spend. That's one of the things that I learned. What I learned beyond that is I have to stay diligent, and every decision I make may not be successful, but I need to understand the process so that I can recover.

Can you share an example of how you have helped a client overcome these obstacles and succeed in using this Principle in their personal or business life?

Johnnie Lloyd: I have two clients who were in the same kind of situation, doing the same thing—one was overspending, the other was not valuing their time. Both of them had the same issue with running out of Money and Time and becoming stressed. We sat down, and one of the things they said is, "We didn't know."

Both were headed towards a brick wall and destruction. Through our training and the things that we helped guide them through, they found an internal peace that allowed them to actually transform their lives. Now, I wrote this book that I use in this case, and titled, "Legacy Moments: Transformation that Goes Beyond Change." What I showed them through this process of learning was using "I am" affirmations and going in and identifying where they are.

One of them ended up with getting more Time so that they could spend time with their family, because they were about to lose everything that they were working hard for, because they were not time-conscious.

The other one was about to lose everything that she had worked hard for, but it was connected to money consciousness. They were in deep debt, so the one goal is coming out of debt is building a savings, which is amazing. Before, they didn't think because she was poverty-conscious, she wasn't wealth-conscious. What ended up happening is that she changed; she transformed her mind to become more wealth-conscious. Not money-conscious, but wealth-conscious.

Now, both of them are on the pathway to having greater success in their personal, private lives. Their relationships are better, and their stress levels are down. The results will work when you work them. So, I would use them both as great examples.

What inspired you to become a Napoleon Hill Certified Leader?

Johnnie Lloyd: I was at an amazing job as an Executive Leader and there was something missing. I was one of those executives that was good at a million things and I did well, very well, but I had not identified my Definite Major Purpose.

I was good at a lot of things and becoming really good at some things, but I was looking for what I was created to do and become great at. Helping people and helping them in this process of becoming greater and finding that sense of purpose, that's my lane because it's the most powerful place. So, I went through the Napoleon Hill Instructor Training and went through the process and all of that, because I was looking for something for me to find out where I was supposed to be great at.

Through that process, I linked back to everything I'd been through in my life. Then I identified it and now I'm just walking it out. It is the most revealing and powerful thing that I've ever done. The reason for that is, I actually did not start the process for others; I started it because I was searching.

However, I continued the process because I really didn't start out to be a Certified Instructor. That was not the intent. But I moved forward after I found it was for me. I said, "Oh, my gosh, this is it." So, I wanted to do it and help other people find that for them.

How do we take this from idea to implementation? What are five steps that people can do right away to start working toward implementing Budgeting Time and Money?

Johnnie Lloyd: The first step is that people need to create a clear mental picture of what they want to do, what they would like, how much money they would like to make, or how much time they need to do something. Identify that. Step zero, if I may add it, is self-awareness. What are you doing now? It's almost like the GPS that I was talking about.

Next, create the vision for where they want to go. Imagine the results of having the money, and/or the time.

The third would be to decide how they're going to earn the money, and the what and the why for earning it—because the why will continue us moving forward when times are rough, and when everything's not going our way.

The next thing is, don't be afraid to fail. Don't be afraid to fail and fail forward. What you do is you fail, you learn, you adjust, and you keep on going. You fail, you learn, you adjust, and you keep on going.

Then you follow that process until you win. Because failing is never final until you stop.

Those would be the five. Then, just to add this last one, is run their race. Don't let society determine what wealth is for you. The person needs to do that as an individual, and not let outside forces be the reason that they want things. Go after wealth as an element of health, their time, their relationship, etc., so that when they can sit on the swing with the person that they care about, at the end of their life, or getting closer to being older, and be that older person, so they're not in the store giving somebody baskets, or having to have to do something that they never anticipated because they weren't prepared.

Are you a female executive or leader who desires to take your life and or organization to the next level? Do you want greater, but there is a gap to getting there? Are you so good at everything but want to know your purpose, your place of greatness? We help guide you into your next level success - from the inside out.

About Johnnie Lloyd

Johnnie is the Chief Visionary Officer and President of Johnnie Lloyd and Associates and successful serial entrepreneur. She is a servant leader who exudes great love and passion for people. Her definite major purpose is to impact lives, especially women in such a way that higher levels of greatest is unleashed.

She is a highly-experienced visionary that specializes in Transformational Development by utilizing proven success principles. She has extensive experience as a Fiscal Executive with over 35 years of expertise. She engages her audiences as a Speaker who has went from homelessness to a builder of wealth. She is a master Facilitator, Coach, Trainer, and Consultant who continues to demonstrate innate ability to facilitate, build, and lead diverse teams to new levels of success in a variety of interactive and engaging ways. Johnnie is a global powerhouse who is a captivating professional with impeccable character and integrity. She is known as a financial Guru "Pusher" who can take financial and other leadership concepts then congruently connect with everyone regardless of their financial background stress, or fears regarding finances. Currently she volunteers training classes and some personalized financial review/coaching for a nonprofit organization that specializes in serving our Veterans in Virginia, providing classes such as Budgeting: Time and Money; Building Self-Confidence; and Self-Discipline.

After retiring to Purpose in 2017 her focus is walking out her definite major purpose. She works from the premise that people are the key to great organizations culture, performance, process, products, and or service. She enjoys creating limitless opportunities for others, based on maximizing their potential through proven principles that are unleashed from right where they are, with what they have. Her motto is "You are fire when you are focused"™ and "Transforming your mind transforms your world and money."

Learn More: www.JohnnieLloyd.com

Principle #17: Cosmic Habitforce – Interview with Amanda Forslund

> *You are the master of your destiny.*
> *You can influence, direct and*
> *control your own environment.*
> *You can make your life what you want it to be.*
> *~Napoleon Hill*

Why is the Principle of Cosmic Habitforce so important today?

Amanda Forslund: The Principle of Cosmic Habitforce is more known as the Law of Attraction. It is relevant for today because it is a Universal Principle. This Principle exists and works no matter if you believe in it or not. It is like gravity - it just exists! Gravitation holds our earth in its proper position and causes all material objects to be attracted toward the center of the earth. In the same way, we are attracting to us that which corresponds with our dominating thoughts. Our thoughts, depending on their nature, attract physical manifestation, because everything what is impressed must be expressed.

This principle will explain how you can acquire habits and how you can adapt yourself to this Universal Principle with the greatest benefit. It works for you in positive or negative way and it depends on how you use it and what are you thinking all day long, because you attract what is your dominant thoughts.

We are ruled by habits, and habits are established by repetition of thoughts and experience. Therefore, we can control our destiny if we can control our thoughts. Humans are the only living creatures who have complete control over their thoughts. If your dominant thoughts are poverty, the Principle translates those thoughts into physical terms of misery and want. Dominant thoughts of abundance translate into their physical counterpart.

Success is the result of being in total harmony with the order, patterns, or habits controlled by this Universal Principle. If you work in harmony with this Principle, you feel flow and ease, but if you work against this Principle, you will be punished. This Principle can be an advantage or a disadvantage, depending on its use. You are the supplier of raw material; you give this Universal Principle the raw material with which to work. It only works with material you give to it. That's why is not important what other people do against you, it is your reaction that counts. Adversity and defeat are a part of the human condition and bad things will happen in your life, but this is only to give you an opportunity to grow and find the seed of equivalent or greater benefit in that defeat. Everyone meets defeat, but as long as you learn something and grow, it is for your benefit. Never doubt that every problem has a solution and that your defeat is just an opportunity to grow!

How does Cosmic Habitforce convert a positive impulse into its physical equivalent? It simply intensifies the desire into a state of mind called Faith and that Faith inspires one to make a plan to achieve the goal. It sets imagination in motion to find most easily available way to converting this desire into money or material things. There is no such a thing as "something for nothing." It depends on your goal, so you need to decide what you are willing to give in return to reach that goal.

What misconceptions are out there surrounding the Principle of Cosmic Habitforce?

Amanda Forslund: A misconception is that people think that this Principle is that it is too easy to be true. I often get this question: "If it is so easy to get what you want, why doesn't everyone use it?" Or I hear: "If everyone gets what he or she wants, that resource will be ended." But that is not the case. The Universe's resources are unlimited. It is like an e-book. You can download it as many times as you want. The same is with a thought - just be careful of what are you downloading to your mind.

Let me tell you how this Principle works. Cosmic Habitforce is the medium through which thoughts are translated into their physical equivalent. First, you create patterns of thought by repeating certain ideas or behavior, and then Cosmic Habitforce takes over those patterns and makes them permanent (depending on the intensity of the repetition) unless or until you consciously rearrange them.

Humans are the only living creature privileged to have a power of choice through which they may establish their own thoughts and habits or break them and rearrange them at will. That's why it is so important to control our thoughts. This Principle can be your best friend, or it can completely demolish your health. Positive thoughts lead to positive emotions and Cosmic Habitforce intensifies that emotion until it induces the state of mind known as Faith. In this state, your mind is receptive to the inflow of Infinite Intelligence, which makes a perfect plan for you, gives you ideas, and makes the right people cross your way. It is up to you to take the opportunity, when it shows. The Universe likes speed, and if you miss the chance, someone else will take it. Nothing is coincidence or luck. Everything is arranged, depending on your dominant thoughts and beliefs. You are the creator of your own future.

What positive changes did you experience in your life after applying the Principle of Cosmic Habitforce to your personal and business life?

Amanda Forslund: A positive change in my life, as a result of knowing how this Principle works, is that it made me aware of my thoughts. I have learned to switch negative thoughts into positive ones, as soon I am aware of them. Now, I don't allow myself to develop a negative thought. It took me a year to learn how, but now I have a tool and can change a negative thought in two seconds. Everyone can learn that because we cannot think two different thoughts at the same time.

Thanks to applying this Principle, I've been released from fears and self-imposed limitations. I have more control over my mind and more control over my life. I am better at interacting with other and live my life with a minimum of friction. My health is better because I don't dwell on things I cannot do anything about. Without negative thoughts in my mind, I feel that every cell in my body is healthy. Applying this Principle clears my mind of negative thoughts and my Faith grows.

Can you share an example of how you have helped a client overcome these obstacles and succeed in using Cosmic Habitforce in their personal or business life?

Amanda Forslund: My daughter was negative and bitter after my divorce and everything she tried to do went wrong. She was almost proud to "have the ability to predict" that everything she started will end up as a failure. I tried to speak to her and explain that she caused all that on her own, but she didn't listen to me. She is my daughter, and I simply don't get it through to her. Then, suddenly, a very nice girl, Pisha, came into our beauty salon where we worked at that time. I supposed that Pisha felt a negative vibration from Zandra, so she told her about the movie, *The Secret,* on YouTube. Zandra was curious because of the name and wanted to know what the secret was, so she checked it out that evening.

You wouldn't believe what happened. The next day, Zandra was a whole new person. She started to think about what she was sending out. She started to fake happiness, smiling to everyone she met, and she was surprised at the response she got. People she met were friendlier and she realized that everything wasn't as dark as she thought. After a while, she wanted to try something bigger, so she decided that she wanted to buy an apartment in Stockholm. She found one apartment she definitely wanted to have, and she started to visualize that she already lived there. She saw in her mind how she went to her new home, put the key in the door, and opened it. She was smiling as she went into the living room, opened the balcony door, and breathed the fresh air. She continued visualizing that every day. Then she tried to get a loan from the bank to buy this apartment. Every bank she went to said "No", but she was determined to get that apartment. She believed in Cosmic Habitforce and knew that she would get what she wants. She had no doubt! Not even for one second! After one week of struggling, she finally got a loan from the bank and could buy that apartment. Most interesting was that not one of those other people who looked at the apartment was interested in it, so she didn't need to pay more money for it.

After this experience, Zandra believed even stronger in Cosmic Habitforce. She still gets everything she wants. It seems to be easy and it is, if you do it in the right way. Never doubt, because if you doubt, you are cancelling your order you just made to the Universe.

What inspired you to become a Napoleon Hill Certified Leader?

Amanda Forslund: I wanted to be a Certified Leader because I realized how powerful those Principles are and I wanted to share them with the whole nation. Napoleon Hill is not as known in Sweden and Croatia as in the USA, and I feel that is my mission to make him and his Principles more known in Europe. Napoleon Hill has done so much for me and I want to give back by continuing his legacy in Europe. Through his Success Principles, I will make an impact on people's lives. I feel honoured to have a license to teach those Principles in both Sweden and Croatia. My goal is to get a license for whole Scandinavia and Balkan countries - and, of course, the island of Cyprus, where I bought a penthouse, thanks to the fact that I came across these principles and started to use them. And to be honest with you, for some selfish reason, too. I want to teach these Principles to others because, when I teach others, I teach myself even more.

What do you think an implementation action plan is for the Principle of Cosmic Habitforce?

Amanda Forslund:

Step 1: Focus on what you want in your life, not what you don't have. Phrase your desires using positive terms. Your thoughts are important. It is starting point of all achievement to really know what you want. Be crystal clear about it.

Step 2: Visualize your goal as already achieved, to intensify what you really want.

Step 3: Meditate on your goal every day until you accomplish it. Learn Saivite meditation. Gather all your energy in your spine, meditate on this particular goal, and then send out energy in your body in a strategic way. I recommend Dandapani's 12-week meditation course.

Step 4: Write down the steps you need to take.

Step 5: Take Action! Do every day one thing which takes you closer to your goal.

About Amanda Forslund

Amanda Forslund is a proud certified instructor of Napoleon Hill's philosophy science of success, business coach, passionate writer and public speaker. Amanda is founder and CEO of Millionaire Mind University a company which works with reprograming the mind, and has developed a training program, *Life by Design* to empower women to find and follow their passion and to reach theirs higher potential.

Previously Amanda had created a 7-figure beauty business in Sweden. Her mission is to continue to promote Napoleon Hill's legacy and spread his proven system of success into Europe. Amanda Forslund is privileged to be the first and only Napoleon Hill's certified instructor in 2019 in both Sweden and Croatia with exclusive right to teach those success principles. She has studied at Brian Tracy's Leadership program, certified at Steven R. Covey's course, *The 7 Good Habits*, and just attend the World Class Speaker 2-years mentorships program with Kane & Alessia Minkus.

But life wasn't always like that. Amanda grew up in the little village of Otok, in Croatia, together with her parents and 12 siblings. She quit school at the age of 14, working at jobs, tired of poverty and with a burning desire to be rich. According the bank account, Amanda still not rich in money, but she is wealthy. She has found peace of mind and inner happiness which she teaches at Millionaire Mind University.

Amanda strongly believes in the potential of individuals, unlimited resources within, and her goal is to empower women to dare to believe in themselves, change their mindset and encourage them to create the life they deserve.

Apart from her professional work, Amanda is a mother, grandmother, has a loving relationship with an amazing gentleman, and lives in Stockholm, Sweden. Amanda loves morning walks in the wood, reading, writing, meditates daily, and travels several times a year to her paradise island of North Cyprus; there she has a beautiful penthouse by the sea.

At www.amandaforslund.com you can find Millionaire Mind University's training program *Life By Design* with the step-by-step guide to get you where you want to be. This program will completely change your mindset and build your courage to dare to believe in yourself, find your passion and live the life you deserve.

Conclusion

After reading the Pathway to a Positive Mental Attitude - 17 Steps to Success Conversations with World-Class Napoleon Hill Certified Leaders, we encourage you to read more of the classics from the Napoleon Hill Foundation and sign up for the motivating Thought for the Day!

https://www.naphill.org/shop/